MODELS OF WORKPLACE TRAINING

MODELS OF WORKPLACE TRAINING

Lessons From the Employees Retraining Scheme

in Hong Kong

Jacqueline Tak-York Cheung

and

Kwong-Leung Tang

Mellen Studies in Business
Volume 9

The Edwin Mellen Press
Lewiston/Queenston/Lampeter

Library of Congress Cataloging-in-Publication Data

Cheung, Jacqueline Tak-York.
  Models of workplace training : lessons from the employees
retraining scheme in Hong Kong / Jacqueline Tak-York Cheung and
Kwong-Leung Tang.
      p. cm - (Mellen studies in business ; v. 9)
  Includes bibliographical references and index.
  ISBN 0-7734-8544-9 (hard)
  1. Occupational retraining--China--Hong Kong--Methodology.
  2. Occupational training--China--Hong Kong--Methodology. I. Tang.
Kwong-Leung. II. Title. II. Series.
HD5715.5.C552H63   1997
331.25'924'095125--dc21   97-29034
                                                                                    CIP

This is volume 9 in the continuing series
Mellen Studies in Business
Volume 9 ISBN 0-7734-8544-9
MSB Series ISBN 0-88946-152-X

A CIP catalog record for this book is available from the British Library.

Copyright © 1997 The Edwin Mellen Press

All rights reserved. For information contact

          The Edwin Mellen Press   The Edwin Mellen Press
                   Box 450   Box 67
            Lewiston, New York   Queenston, Ontario
            USA 14092-0450   CANADA L0S 1L0

                          The Edwin Mellen Press, Ltd.
                          Lampeter, Dyfed, Wales
                          UNITED KINGDOM SA48 7DY

                  Printed in the United States of America

DEDICATION

To all industrial workers who have struggled hard in Hong Kong

TABLE OF CONTENTS

CHAPTER   **PAGE**

♦ ♦ ♦

TABLES

PREFACE

This book presents an analysis of the current state of workplace training in Hong Kong. While models of workplace training in the industrialized nations have received a great deal of attention and been subjected to very critical appraisal, labor retraining in developing nations has not received the attention it deserves. This is disappointing since a number of developing nations have implemented different forms of labor training programs. The intent of this book is to document the development of the Employees Retraining Scheme of Hong Kong and the problems it has encountered. Given the handover of Hong Kong to the Chinese government in 1997, discussion of current labor training policy is useful to form a backdrop against which future development can be compared.

The main line of argument of this book is that a behavioral model of training has been accepted uncritically and unwittingly by the Hong Kong government. Many problems have thus ensued. Before the analysis of Hong Kong, we have devoted considerable discussion to the analysis of workplace training models in North America. Behavioral models emerged in North America at a time when they were well matched to the dominant concept of Taylorism in management. These models put a strong emphasis on classroom-based and formal group activities and discourage or minimize worker participation. However, this approach is now increasingly challenged by the worker-centered models. Four factors are contributing to

v

this change; social changes, new needs of capitalism, the importance of worker ownership and attitudinal changes in management. Three emerging alternatives to the behavioral approach include those based on Action Regulation Theory, critical reflectivity and "working-class adult education" approaches.

The relative merits of these approaches have not really been explored in Hong Kong's Employees Retraining Scheme, in spite of the possible virtues of doing so. Instead, contrary to its long-standing non-intervention position in labor market, the Hong Kong government rather reactively set up an Employees Retraining Scheme in 1992 to provide retraining for displaced workers. Some socio-political and economic factors (economic restructuring, market failures, policy linkages, corporatist structure of government, international division of labor) account for this action. In addition, this program is seen as strongly connected to the General Labour Importation Scheme and as a compromise on the part of government to harmonize the interests of workers and employers. As a corollary, this expedient and half-hearted program which aims at reconciling conflicting interests faces a number of drawbacks. They include: a lack of vision, a mismatch between jobs and skills training, and the absence of long-term strategy.

Above all, based on a number of criteria generated from a survey of theories of workplace learning (objectives of training, focus of training, format of learning, participation of workers, construction of knowledge and concept of management), it is seen that the new scheme adopts a behavioral model of learning. This fits well with the expedient nature of the program and the top-down, bureaucratic nature of the program's development. The emphasis is on the adoption of new skills, not enhancing learning capacity. It seems dubious that this narrow focus on skills training prepares workers for the challenge of changing and varied work environments. This short-sightedness is the Achilles' heel of the whole program. It is in an effort to clarify the nature and specific instances of this short-sightedness so as to improve retraining in Hong Kong that we offer this critique of the program to date.

◆　　◆　　◆

ACKNOWLEDGEMENTS

We have accumulated many debts over the time it has taken us to write this book. Since parts of this book are taken from a thesis which Jacqueline submitted to the Department of Education, University of British Columbia, we are extremely grateful to Professor Kjell Rubenson of the University of British Columbia for his consistent support and reassurance. His expertise had first broadened and deepened our understanding of the area of study. We are deeply indebted to a number of people in Hong Kong and especially to Andy Cheung, Jacob Cheung, Apo Po-lam Leung, and Fung-Ngor Luk for their assistance in data collection. Thanks are due to our close friends Rachel Day and Isabelle Harris, who helped in the editing of the first draft. Their comments have been immensely useful in improving the quality of this research. The standard disclaimer applies: any remaining errors are the sole responsibility of the authors.

The most important information has come from discussions with concerned personnel who are involved in the program, either as education administrators, labor union organizers or trainees. Their assistance was invaluable to our study. They have provided us with updated information, course contents, administration papers and program proposals. Last but not least, feedback from trainees was collected through several structured interviews of trainees who have participated in different training courses, survey reports from labor organizations and letters to editors of major Chinese newspapers in Hong Kong. We are deeply indebted to all our sources.

The main chapters of this book were written in 1994 but history does not stand still. Since then, because the Employee Retraining Scheme has undergone several changes, we have updated the chapters in the light of these changes. A book that attempts to cover workplace retraining in Hong Kong over the last five years is likely to be wanting in some respects. We hope, however, that others will take up the challenge of both conceptualising and providing a solid base for the exploration of appropriate and sound models of workplace training for East Asia and other developing countries.

Finally, thanks are due Taylor and Francis Press. Parts of the first two chapters (with some modifications) have appeared in: Kwong-leung Tang and Jacqueline Tak-york Cheung, 1996, "Models of Workplace Training in North America: A Review." *International Journal of Lifelong Education*, Volume 15, Number 4, pages 256-65, copyright @ 1996 by Taylor and Francis Press, United Kingdom.

◆ ◆ ◆

Vancouver, British Columbia   Kwong-leung Tang
January, 1997   Jacqueline Tak-york Cheung

CHAPTER ONE

WORKPLACE TRAINING
AND DEVELOPMENT

Workplace training and development is a rapidly developing field of practice in adult education. It is well-documented that throughout the world both government and the private sector devote substantial resources to enhancing work-related learning for employees.[1] For example, in the United States, the American Society of Training and Development[2] reported that $210 billion is spent by the business sector each year on formal and non-formal learning, compared to $144 billion for elementary and secondary education. In the same period, the U. S. Government also spent some $5 billion in training. Indeed, between 1983 and 1991, there was a 17 percent increase in the number of employees who reported receiving skill-improvement training while in their current jobs. Some 37 percent of this training occurred at the workplace.[3] When types of training are taken into consideration, the greatest emphasis seems to be on management, supervisory, new-employee orientation, and technical skills. Such policies also occur in Canada. Although in Canada, education is a provincial responsibility, the federal government is heavily committed to the training and development of the labor force for economic growth and full employment. It is estimated that approximately $11 billion is spent annually by the federal government for this purpose.[4]

Not surprisingly, similar efforts are noted throughout Europe. In Britain, there has been a substantial amount of training. The Training Agency[5] estimated that the overall cost of training in 1986-87 was £33 billion. Labor Force Survey data show 9.1 percent of all employees had received training in the last four weeks of 1984; by 1990 this figure had reached 15.4 percent. Economists have worked out that Britain has spent some ten percent of its gross domestic product on training. A general picture of training in Britain has emerged: larger firms are more likely to provide training than smaller firms, training declines with age, training is more concentrated in service industries than in manufacturing, and the public sector provides more training than the private sector.[6]

In other countries undertaking significant training which were identified in a recent study,[7] a variety of measures reveal the impact of training. For example, France has a specific legislation to ensure training monies. It has a law requiring enterprises to spend a defined percentage of their total wage bill (1.1 percent in 1985) for training purposes. This includes training for employees, which enables them to acquire skills for new jobs (0.1 percent), and provides for the initial training of young people (0.2 percent). In the Federal Republic of Germany, comparative studies between 1979 and 1985 show that the percentage of gainfully employed persons without apprenticeship or vocational school training declined from 28 percent (1979) to 21 percent (1985), and the participation rate of gainfully employed persons in further vocational training or retraining increased from 15 percent (1979) to 17 percent (1985). In Sweden, a number of laws have been promulgated and collective agreements concluded which relate to the training of workers. This has been part of a substantial industrial restructuring during the last ten to fifteen years. In Japan, there has been an increase in the number of employees receiving on-the-job training, from 76.7 percent in 1976 to 82.5 percent in 1984.

Models of Workplace Training

The experience of a number of workplace training programs indicates a definite relationship between the provision of employee skills programs and increased worker productivity.[8] Despite all the importance attached to workplace training, however, most training programs operated by governments in North America have either very little or no worker participation. Instead, the dominant training model uses a basic behavioral approach, designed to meet the needs of organizations after World War II. Much of its early application came from military experience, i.e., in organizations whose predominant mode of operation was like a machine. Training was thus oriented to behavioral outcomes that could be measured. This has evolved into a practice today in which training and workers' education are governed by an organizational ideal of a well-functioning machine with clear hierarchical lines of authority.

In spite of its narrow focus, however, the prevailing behavioral model has contributed to improving productivity in many instances. It works most effectively in situations when there is only one right answer to a problem and that answer calls for an expert-based solution. It promotes uniformity of action and clarification of what learners need to do to satisfy employers' requests. It makes learning manageable by focusing on specific objectives, and upholds minimum organizational standards.[9]

Recently, this behavioral model has come under strong challenge from some alternative perspectives. It is criticized as inadequate to meet the developmental needs of workers in many conditions. Another serious problem is that such models exclude workers except as recipients.[10] To be sure, those who support a worker-centered approach see a central role for the workers in developing the training programs. One would assume that if a system of lifelong learning that provides relevant skills to all is to be established, then workers themselves should have a central role in developing the programs.[11] Bringing workers back into the center stage of training programs has been the key proposition of early approaches to adult education. For example, in the tradition of the humanistic school, Knowles[12] has put forth an alternative collaborative approach to adult learning — Andragogy. And there have been many other demands for a more work-centered approach in the assembly line.

In short, a plethora of new approaches have cropped up. But it would be fair to say the behavioral model never loses much ground, although the ramifications of this model are increasingly criticized. Thus, there is a clear need to examine and compare the dominant behavioral model against other new models, as an aid to our understanding of the industrial and social environments and as a basis for policy changes. Although such examination has been substantial in developed nations, it has not been conducted in the context of developing countries. One reason is that not many developing countries have comparable programs of workers' training;

another is that the careful scrutiny of the behavioral model undertaken even in advanced nations is relatively recent.

Given the predominance of the behavioral model in the industrialized countries, it is reasonable to generalize that the same model would be applied in developing countries, particularly those high-income ones which have paid some attention to workers' training in order to enhance their competitiveness in the world market. The four East Asian Newly Industrializing Countries (NICs) of Hong Kong, Singapore, South Korea and Taiwan are relevant here, since they are especially receptive to the diffusion of western ideas and influences. It would be erroneous to assume that other high-income developing countries in Asia seldom embark upon training programs. A case in point is Singapore. Like Hong Kong, Singapore is also a city-state committed to export-led industrialization. However, unlike Hong Kong, it started very early in the retraining of workers. The Skills Development Levy Act of 1979 established a fund to which employers contributed a levy equal to two percent of the monthly remuneration of every employee earning S$750 and below. This was increased to four percent in July 1980, reduced to two percent in April 1985 and eventually dropped to one percent in 1986. The 1995 target was to get employers to invest four percent of their total annual payroll in training. For their part, employers, unions, and individuals can apply to the Skills Development Fund for partial or full refund if they need to use any of the training approved by the Skills Development Fund.[13]

Certainly, it will be pertinent to study their models for workers' training, including their inception and resulting problems. Given the large number of developing countries, it is more feasible to choose those countries which have implemented some forms of training programs and whose political and economic features are amenable to scrutiny. In our study, we decided to look specifically at the case of Hong Kong, as it has recently introduced a retraining program for workers.

Retraining Program in Hong Kong

Hong Kong is a British colony which is scheduled to return to China after 1997. For a long time, the colonial government has adopted a laissez-faire policy in its economic development. Official intervention in the field of labor training has been minimal. But the government decided in 1992 to foster a retraining program for displaced workers, especially for those sectors in which labor shortages are the most serious. The government thus approved spending some HK$300 million (US$38 million) for the program. Priority has been given to workers aged above 30 but below 55 and currently unemployed or underemployed. The latter category includes those who involuntarily work less than 34 hours a week and who are seeking more work, or who are available for additional work. Working short hours is deemed "involuntary" if it is due to economic reasons which include slack work, material shortages, or inability to find full-time work.

Pursuing a free enterprise economy for over one hundred and fifty years, the Hong Kong government has never been very active in labor training. Instead, that responsibility has been taken up by independent boards working in collaboration with major employers' associations to run vocational training programs. Hence, the new retraining program mentioned above is rather unique as it represents strong intervention on the part of the government, considerable organization, and governmental financial commitment in the sphere of the workplace for the first time.

It is the intent of this book to look into the following questions:

1. What are the economic, social or political forces which shape the formation of this retraining program? Under what influences has the Hong Kong government decided to pursue this program?

2. Looking at the contents and implementation of the retraining program, what models of learning are used? Is the behavioral model adopted? If so, how does the model work in practice?

3. Can the training model achieve its objectives of training and industrial redeployment? Are there problems which hinder its goal realization? Are they attributable to the use of the behavioral model?

Organization of this Book

This study focuses on the labor training model chosen for the new employment training scheme in Hong Kong. In order to understand it fully, the next chapter reviews various models of workplace learning to highlight some important characteristics of the models. These in turn will provide some criteria for analyzing the case of workplace training in Hong Kong. The identification of these criteria paves the groundwork for an analytic model to study the case of Hong Kong.

Hong Kong's socio-political and economic backgrounds for the retraining program are explored in Chapter Three, followed by a description of the objectives and structure of the new employment training program.

Specifically, the influences of social, economic, and political forces on workplace learning in the context of Hong Kong are examined. A more detailed analysis of the implementation of the program, based on the indicators developed in Chapter Two, is given in Chapter Four. In Chapter Five, the effectiveness of the program is assessed. Chapter Six concludes with a summary of the most up-to-date information regarding the scheme as of time of publication.

This study is based on fieldwork carried out by the researchers in Hong Kong. The bulk of the research was carried out in 1994; however, we have sought to update specific changes that have taken place between then and the time of publication. Much of the information and many of the statistics cited in the first two chapters come from official documents such as the *Hong Kong Annual Report, Employees Retraining Ordinance*, reports and publications of the Employees Retraining Board, and minutes and notes of the Hong Kong Legislative Council. Insights into the program have also been gained through references from literature, a review of labor training in Hong Kong, survey reports, newsletters of labor organizations, newspaper clippings, letters to editors, and annual reports of various training bodies. The most important and valuable information, however, has come from discussions with concerned personnel who are involved in the program, either as education administrators, labor union organizers or trainees. In particular, we managed to interview (through a structured questionnaire) five trainees who shared their experiences with us in early 1994.

◆   ◆   ◆

NOTES

1. Carnevale, Anthony (1989). "Workplace Basics: The Skills Employers Want." *AACJC Journal*, Feb/March, pp. 29-33. Carnevale, A. & Ferman, L. (Eds.) (1990). *New Developments in Worker Training: A Legacy for the 1990s*. Madison, WI: Industrial Relations Research Association. Carnevale, Anthony & Carnevale, Ellen S. (1994). "Growth Patterns in Workplace Training." *Training and Development, 48*, pp. 22-28.

2. American Society for Training and Development (1986). *Serving The New Corporation*. Alexandria, VA: Author. American Society for Training and Development (1994). "The Coming of Age of Workplace Learning: A Time Line." *Training and Development, 48*, pp. 4-21.

3. Carnevale, A. and E. Carnevale (1994). "Growth Patterns in Workplace Training."

4. Human Resources Development Canada (1994). *Agenda: Jobs and Growth: Improving Social Security in Canada. A Discussion Paper*. Ottawa: Minister of Supply and Services.

5. Training Agency (1989). *Defining the Demographic Time Bomb*. London: National Economic Development Office.

6. Shackleton, J. R. (1992). *Training Too Much?* London: Institute of Economic Affairs.

7. International Labor Organization (1991). *Workers' Education in Action: Selected Articles from Labour Education*. Geneva: International Labour Office.

8. Business Council for Effective Literacy (1993). *The Connection Between Employee Basic Skills and Productivity*. New York: BCEL Brief.

9. Marsick, V. J. (1988a). Learning in the Workplace: The Case for Reflectivity and Critical Reflectivity." *Adult Education Quarterly 38* (4), pp. 187-98. Marsick, V. J. (1988b). *Enhancing Staff Development in Diverse Settings*. San Francisco: Jossey-Bass.

10. Sarmiento, A. R. and A. Kay (1990). *Worker-centered Learning: A Union Guide to Workplace Literacy*. Washington: AFL-CIO Human Resources Development Institute.

11.   Marsick, V. J. and K. Watkins (1990). *Information and Incidental Learning in the Workplace*. New York: Routledge. Sefton, R. (1993). "An Integrated Approach to Training in the Vehicle Manufacturing Industry in Australia." *Critical Forum*, 2(2), pp. 39-51.

12.   Knowles, M. (1980). *From Pedagogy to Andragogy*. Chicago: Follett Publishing Company.

13.   Yun, Hing Ai (1995). "Automation and the New Work Patterns: Cases from Singapore's Electronics Industry." *Work, Employment and Society*, Vol. 9, No. 2, pp. 309-27.

CHAPTER TWO

AN OVERVIEW OF
WORKPLACE TRAINING MODELS

The conflict between those who support a worker-centered training strategy and those who opt for a management-centered one represents the continuation of theoretical tension between positivism and humanism in adult education. As argued by Bhola,[1] positivism is marked by the following features: training by objectives, an emphasis on competence, a focus on content, and the role conception of animator and facilitator. By contrast, humanism focuses on human beings and their values, capacities and achievements. These two orientations are by no means mutually exclusive. Yet in most cases, the positivist point of view has been dominant in training of skills.

With regard to the history of workplace learning, it is no surprise to see that the positivistic orientation had received early and widespread support. It has been the dominant view adopted by many employers in skills training. The traditional view of learning in the workplace is based on behaviorism.[2] The behavioral model presupposes a production orientation, and aims at training people for machine-like work according to their levels in a hierarchy such as an assembly line.

The Dominant Paradigm: The Behavioral Model

Marsick[3] has summarized the characteristics of the current behavioristic paradigm for workplace learning:

1. Emphasis on behaviorally-oriented and performance outcomes which can be observed, quantified and criterion-reference.

2. Separation of personal and work-related development.

3. Matched to organizational ideal of a well-functioning machine with clear, hierarchical lines of authority, jobs that do not overlap, and rational systems of delegation and control.

4. Aimed at meeting needs of individuals, not groups.

5. Emphasis on objectivity, rationality and step-by-step procedures in problem solving.

6. Training conducted primarily in form of classroom-based and formal group activities.

7. Focused on "pure" learning problems and manipulation of the work environment to sustain outcomes.

8. Learning conceived on a "deficit" model that measures individuals against standard, expert-derived norms.

The behavioral model is very well matched to the dominant concept of management in America known as "Taylorism." The roots of this concept can be traced back to the work of Frederick Taylor, an American, in the last century. It has been refined and developed to meet contemporary needs. It made its greatest impact on the world at large during and after the Second World War when the United States emerged as an economic super-power. Briefly speaking, the objective of the Taylorism is to treat work and management in a "scientific" manner. This system requires a separation between the planning function and the execution function of the production process in the workplace. Planning and organizing work is the responsibility of the management level: managers are responsible for all decision making, problem solving and quality control activities. By contrast, work tasks are broken down into their smallest elements and become fairly clearly defined sequences of operations to be performed by individuals. Once the workers have learned the sequences of operations, they simply repeat the tasks on a continuous basis and refer to their supervisors or management levels for any problems. All problems are solved by management specialists such as production engineers, quality engineers, work-study engineers and production control engineers. These specialists totally control the work process. The Americans used this "scientific system" to build their massive armament machine during the Second World War and later, to flood world markets with cheap mass-produced goods. This impressed other industrialized countries and the system spread quickly to other parts of the world.

The organizational structures under the Taylor system of management favor the adoption of a behavioral model in workplace training. The behavioral scientists have proved that their model is very efficient in cases where workers are trained to take up a precise technique which allows no variation. However, various factors have arisen which undermine the effectiveness of this management system and confound the behaviorist training model: social change, new needs of capitalism, worker ownership and attitudinal changes. The result has been a mushrooming of new and alternative concepts of management and new models of workplace learning. Before looking at these new models, what goes wrong for the behavioral model has to be put in proper perspective.

Social Change

The behavioral model of training was formulated to meet societal needs after World War II, when organizational structures were centralized and standardized, mass production was assumed, educational levels of workers were low, and technology was primitive. There have been great changes since them. Different demands have to be met if the present-day business is to survive and flourish in the post-industrial technological era. Pressures to change come from the external world of business (especially the technological revolution), the increase in international competition, and the nature of the workforce itself. Carnevale and Goldstein[4] highlight some additional economic factors which require adjustments to the Taylorist model: the impact of the baby boom generation and women entering the marketplace in large numbers, a large pool of both more highly-educated minorities and immigrants, and the phenomenon of the mid-career glut.

New Needs of Capitalism

A radical view of training/retraining sees it as a business in adult education which is experiencing dramatic growth as corporations shut down plants or move them to different countries where labor can be more readily exploited.[5] The need for training/retraining has changed dramatically. As a result, adjustments are clearly needed and workers' training has acquired a new face, which allows more focus on the workers. Some researchers even regard training/retraining as a "growth industry." New rhetoric in workers' education has even emerged, including such catchwords as "problem solver," "communication skills," "thinking skills," and "lifelong learning." Noble[6] seems to have a clear understanding of this post-industrial trend in retraining:

> workers might even be considered "highly skilled," so long as they are an adaptable cog, a flexible processing unit, in high performance technological systems that meet the needs of capital at the present movement.

Worker Ownership

Since the mid-1970s, American workers have been buffeted by waves of plant closures, relocations, intensified foreign competitive, and corporate mergers.[7] One popular response to these events has been the worker buy-out. There are two legal forms for this: a worker's cooperative or an employee stock ownership plan. Although the educational needs of these two modes of control are different, they call for a greater fusion between management and active involvement of workers. There is thus a trend towards worker democracy and the need for overcoming the lack of skills, confidence and experience among the "worker owners."

Attitudinal Changes

The dehumanizing aspects of old organization structures designed along Taylorist principles are increasingly held responsible, and subsequently challenged, for low self-confidence and morale among the workers. Changes are thus being explored which place increased emphases on intangible factors in production and management. These include: human values, new forms of social interaction, commitment, a service orientation, risk-taking, independent thinking, integration among units within the organization as well as in external interfaces, and creativity.

In sum, management has had to redefine productivity goals while short-term profit-taking has necessarily been mediated by a longer-term perspective on forms of productivity which capitalize on creativity and human resources.

Emerging Paradigm

Dissatisfaction with the behavioral model has, therefore, led to the rise of a number of alternative training models. As seen, early challenge comes from the humanistic school of Knowles who puts forth a student-centered approach to adult learning — Andragogy. Knowles proposes a student-centered approach to adult learning which, in workplace training, translates into a worker-centered approach to assembly line training, including propositions of lifelong learning for workers. Sticht and Hickey[8] maintain the biological make-up of human beings and the contexts in which they function determine what will be learned, how it will be learned, and how the learning will be transferred. From this, they develop their Functional Context Theory based on an extensive review of worker training. Kornbluh and Greene[9] call for non-formal education which is a synthesis of empowerment learning theory and Knowles' work. Their model emphasizes developing "learning enabler roles," organizations as learning milieus, meaningful participatory processes, and a work climate committed to worker learning.

There are many other models which crop up to challenge the behavioral model. Three models or approaches are especially relevant to discuss here: Action Regulation Theory, a "critical reflectivity approach," and "working-class adult education" approach. The first two models place strong emphasis on participation of workers and the third is a British attempt to synthesize adult education with labor education. Strictly speaking, such an approach is not new; rather it is a restatement of the importance of workers' interests and perspectives in labor education. Together, these approaches constitute the outlines of a new paradigm of training. However, it is still in formation. Nevertheless, its focus is notable: it is one of learning, not training or education.

(1) Action Regulation Theory

This theory provides a particular view on human development and the impact of work conditions on personality. It is constructed around two frames: models of evolution and self-organizing systems, and theories concerning society and relations between individuals and society. The theory starts with an analysis of a person's learning process. A central assumption is that a person strives for autonomy in action in order to satisfy a basic control or need. A motivated and autonomous-oriented individual sets goals and reaches them. These processes are the psychological aspect of action referred as a "regulation." The translation of a general goal into a sequence of operations occurs through a hierarchical-sequential organization of actions.

There are different levels of action units differentiated by levels of regulation that determines the scope of action. Thus, regulation chances are important determinants of an individual's socialization process and personal development. If a person is denied the chance of exercising autonomy in these choices, he is incapable of learning more elaborate actions, which in turn adversely affects his motivation and competencies. This is called "restrictive regulation requirements." A major prescription from the proponents of Action Regulation Theory is to increase regulation requirements and remove regulation barriers. Applied to the workplace, this suggests increased opportunities for workers to participate.

Several researchers have sought to apply this theory to workplace training. Volpert[10] suggests that there are three principles that guide learning in the workplace: (1) the learning process must refer to different levels of regulation. It is an integrated one since there is no hard boundary between acquisition of skill and acquisition of knowledge; (2) to ensure and enhance the flexibility of action schema, learners need to be confronted with varying situations and different action demands; and (3) the learning process must be aligned to a high level of learner self-reliance.

These three principles are paralleled by three types of cognitive training. These include: (1) heuristic rules that help one to internalize the rules as action guides; (2) self-instruction which combines well-structured learning materials with forms of self-instruction; and (3) task-oriented information exchanges where workers discuss the problems and solutions of complex work tasks.

In practice, Action Regulation Theory has inspired much of the Swedish experiments in workers' participation. Specifically, the theory has also given support to its labor movement's struggle for humanization of work, workplace democracy, and the more equitable distribution of knowledge in society. In their study of application of Action Regulation Theory in Sweden, Rubenson and Schutze[11] have formulated the following theses from their study of new work organization and the application of action regulation to the workplace.

First, the changes in work organization and technology have called for a broader range of educational activities. There is a corresponding need to reintegrate learning and work in the workplace. Also, workplaces need to be understood as learning environments whereby individuals acquire knowledge, experience, creativity, and sense of responsibility. Third, there should be a close association between humanization of work and the principles of effective learning. Fourth, a new emphasis should be put on informal learning, as these researchers found that exposure to all types of learning situations increases the motivation of workers. Clearly such research reveals a marked contrast to the behavioral model of workplace training.

(2) Critical Reflectivity Perspective

Relying on Habermas' theory of communication competence, Mezirow[12] developed a theory of adult learning. In this characterization, human learning is divided into two interactive domains: the instrumental and the communicative, with an additional dimension of reflective learning. Instrumental learning is concerned with task-oriented problem solving, communicative learning refers to seeking an understanding or consensus with others, and reflectivity involves examining the assumptions and premises of either domain. The underlying assumption is that adults cannot separate learning for organization productivity from learning for personal growth. According to this theory, an organization with employees capable of critical reflection is the one best suited to respond to challenges of changing environments and competition.

Drawing upon Mezirow's work and action science, Marsick and her associates[13] formulated a "critical reflectivity" model of workplace learning. The main characteristics are as follows:

1. Work-related learning is most productive when workers can participate fully in negotiating their contribution to shared organizational goals and norms and they feel that work is personally meaningful.

2. Workers learn best about the jobs when their own identity and growth are recognized as integral to that learning.

3. Workers are encouraged to learn to participate in appropriate decentralized decision-making, and continually monitor actions and results to keep the organization flexible.

4. Learning design emphasizes critical reflectivity.

5. Teamwork is emphasized as a basis for creating working goals and work relationships.

6. There is a focus on problem setting and problem solving.

7. Informal learning is emphasized.

8. Overall, the organization is considered as a learning environment for the growth of individuals and groups vis-à-vis work.

Clearly, there are strong similarities between Marsick's perspective and Action Regulation Theory in practice despite different emphases in their frameworks. Both recommend greater worker participation and power in decision-making. In view of that, the emerging paradigm is referred to as "worker-centered" approach in this study when it is compared to the paradigm of behaviorism. Moreover, examples of this worker-centered approach are growing in number. Marsick[14] has discussed three examples: New York City's Department of Sanitation which has fostered a culture of learning; the M. Price Corporation which strives for a training for service orientation; and the Management Institute in Lund, Sweden which has introduced action learning in the workplace.

(3) "Working-Class Adult Education" Approach

Another approach seeks to establish critical linkages between adult education and workers' education.[15] Recently, Fryer[16] outlined the agenda for working-class adult education which in essence is a search for enlightenment. No doubt this approach would decry the functional-technical emphases embodied in the behavioral model of workers' training. A key feature of the agenda is that the purpose of adult education for workers is to stimulate constructive thought and inspiration to action. Adult education is regarded as inseparable from the human struggle for freedom and dignity, equality and justice. Thus the focus of effective workers' education is a critical and creative analysis of social, political, economic and technological life in modern society. Its character is both practical and analytical. It draws creatively upon experience, including the "experiences of oppression and exploitation," with a view to synthesizing personal reflection with theoretical and conceptual insights "to transcend the otherwise obvious threat of a mere reproduction of the language and conditions of subordination."[17]

The method of such education is one of active promotion of worker involvement in curriculum negotiation and study. Again, this approach, with its overt aims of supra-organizational change with individuals and collective enlightenment, is markedly different from the functional technical emphases embodied in the behavioral approach.

Limitations of the New Models

Admittedly, the emerging paradigm of workplace training has gained much support even from some employers. As discussed, the Scandinavian model of work organization has been successful in many respects. For instance, in Norway and Sweden, extensive research in the 1960s and 1970s showed that those workers who actively engaged in decision-making in their workplaces and work environments were least likely to suffer occupational injury and illness. Such activation was found to be conducive to continuously improve the work environment.[18] Further, Rubenson and Schutze[19] have argued that quality circles, which have proven to be successful in Japanese industries, can be interpreted as an example of applied Action Regulation Theory.

However, the emerging paradigm still encounters a number of problems. First, workplace learning will always be governed by an instrumental focus because the primary goal for organizations is productivity, not employee education. Second, some individuals are not ready to participate more fully in decision-making and self-directed learning. Ravid[20] observes that even when one is ready to implement a self-directed learning approach, consensus is needed on its meaning and strategies for implementation. This process could be both expensive and confusing, unless done properly. Third, organizations cannot always change conditions such as hierarchy and centralized decision-making even when they wish to do so. Lastly, in western countries, the kind of participative behaviors advanced by the emerging paradigm may often be met with resistance, since it challenges existing divisions of labor.

There are many other blocks to developing educative work environments. The first hindrance is related to the artificial and rigid divisions of many workplace professions, which clearly hinders knowledge flow. Work is split into "knowing," "doing," and "being." Workforces are assigned mainly to "doing," support staffs are assigned to "knowing," and executives to "being" the organization. Another split is between labor, planning, and action; workers labor, staffs design, and managers act.[21]

Further, some critical issues remain to be researched. It is unclear how workers involved in micro-level technology decision-making could carry those experiences into an expanded macro-level perspective. For instance, workers might just be involved in the design or implementation of new technology on the job. There might not be opportunities for workers to involve at the enterprise level. Since important technology decisions are made at the corporate level and tied to national economic policy-making, it is necessary for workers to relate their local participation experiences to these broader issues.[22]

Criteria for Worker-Centered Models

In the above, three models with different views on how adults learn are presented. An area which needs to be addressed is the difference between a model of learning in the workplace and what might be described as philosophy of education. The choice between the two involves more than accepting a theory of human learning; it also involves values and assumptions about the appropriate function of adult education in the workplace. Obviously, proponents of those models have to find additional and stronger justifications for their applications in real life.

To summarize, there have been demands for better qualified workers in face of global competition in economy. Different models of learning in the workplace not only dictate different approaches, but also reflect conflicting values concerning human and structural agencies. It is most essential for adult educators to be certain of their roles in workers' education through critical reflection on the philosophy of adult education.

As noted, three models of workplace training with different views on how adults learn are discussed. They all have different emphases but they also have something in common. They believe that the following considerations are important in workplace training:

1. Learning from experience — People learn from and through their experiences as well as making sense of new situations by applying what they have learned in the past. Training, therefore, must be built upon people's experiences in order to be meaningful.

2. Importance of context — The context in which workers function determines to a great extent how they make their decisions. Even in a highly technical environment, decisions are often dependent on the judgement of people who tend to refer to external frames of reference. The external context can be cultural, social or political.

3. Action and Reflection — It bridges the gap between theories espoused and theories in-use and helps people to understand underlying variables governing their actions. It leads to critical thinking which is important in all learning.

4. Learning to learn — The changing economy, the rapid advances in technology and the demands of organizations require a workforce that is analytical, adaptive, and innovative. The skills of learning-to-learn which enable workers to possess new information and acquire coping strategies should be the most fundamental and basic component in workplace learning.

5. Worker as a Learner — People have different learning needs and learn in different styles. Further, the learning process is affected by the learners' personal, social, organizational and cultural beliefs. The trainers have to possess good understanding about the characteristics of a training group in order to carry out an effective program.

In short, the new paradigms are more worker-oriented and experience-based. Worker training is no longer limited to the adoption of specific skills or knowledge as required by a job. Attention is now paid to the workers' developmental needs as well as cognitive and effective components of learning. Workers are regarded as human beings who are open to various social and environmental influences. Further, workplace learning is not regarded as an one-time change in behavior. Training in job skills is an ongoing process and workers need to develop their skills to initiate learning. All these concepts have moved a long way from the traditional behavioral model.

As noted, these newer approaches to workplace training are very different, though they may not be entirely mutually exclusive, from the behavioral model. The differences are particularly important in the following areas:

1.   Objectives of training — The behavioral approach is very job or skills specific. The aim is to being about change in job performance in specific posts. By contrast, the new models emphasize basic skills and learning capacity of workers. Abilities to analyze, reflect and think critically are regarded as essential. Hence, the ultimate objective in the newer approach is to develop a proactive and creative work team.

2.   Focus of training — The behavioral approach is rather task-oriented. Results are measured by observable data or better control of cause-effect actions. The new paradigms, however, focus more on basic skills and problem-solving abilities. Besides these generic skills, workers are expected to understand more about their field of work, be more critical about the taken-for-granted practices, and more able to apply their knowledge to meet new demands in their jobs.

3.   Construction of knowledge — The behavioral model regards knowledge as objective and concrete, and transmittable from authority, i.e., experts to the workers. Attitudes are considered important only in terms of how they can be manipulated to motivate and sustain changes in behavior. The new paradigms are more experience-based and context-oriented. Concepts like proactive learning, self-directed learning, and collaborative learning are based

on the assumption that knowledge construction is a process through which people generate meanings out of their actions or interactions with the environment.

4. Participation of workers — In the traditional model of workplace training, workers are passive recipients of knowledge. The new trend places them in a very active and central role, as well as at different levels of participation, from problem identification to program design and classroom participation. Moreover, the participation style moves from mainly individual to group, due to the recognition of the importance of teamwork and social interactions in the workplace.

5. Format of training — Formal classroom training is often adopted in the behavioral model. The work environment is considered as critical in sustaining changed behavior, but the workers have no control over it. The new models propose a more egalitarian framework instead of a hierarchical line of authority. Theories like Action Regulation uphold the importance of workers having control over their learning contexts.

6. Concept of Management — The traditional model is most compatible with the image of organization as a mechanical, hierarchical system in which people are placed and fitted into different clearly defined units of the system to make it run smoothly. The new models interpret organization with a more people-centered philosophy. It is more dynamic, interactive, and collaborative. The organization itself is liable to be reconceived by people who would challenge and

change the norms when encountering new demands in the greater environment.

These criteria, which reveal such basic differences between the traditional and more recent approaches to workplace training, serve as good indicators with which to discuss the Employees Retraining Scheme in Hong Kong. We will return to them in Chapter Four, after a discussion of some cultural and historical contexts of employment training in Hong Kong.

NOTES

1. Bhola, H. S. (1988). *World Trends and Issues in Adult Education.* United Nations: UNESCO.

2. Marsick, V. J. (Ed.) (1987). *Learning in the Workplace.* Kent, U.K.: Croom Helm.

3. Marsick, V. J. (1988a). "Learning in the Workplace: The Case for Reflectivity and Critical Reflectivity." *Adult Education Quarterly 38*(4), 187-98. Marsick, V. J. (1988b). *Enhancing Staff Development in Diverse Settings.* San Francisco: Jossey-Bass.

4. Carnevale A. and H. Goldstein (1983). *Employee Training: Its Changing Role and An Analysis of New Data.* Washington, D.C.: ASTD Press.

5. Noble, D. D. (1990). "High-Tech Skills: The Latest Corporate Assault on Workers" in S. H. London, T. R. Tarr and F. J. Wilson (Eds.) *The Re-education of the American Working Class*, pp. 131-44. New York: Greenwood.

6. Noble, D. D. *High-Tech Skills*, p. 142.

7. Hellyer, M. R. and B. Schulman (1989). "Workers' Education." in S. B. Merriam and P. M. Cunningham (Eds.), *Handbook of Adult and Continuing Education*, pp. 569-83. San Francisco: Jossey-Bass.

8. Sticht, T. G. and D. T. Hickey (1991). "Functional Context Theory, Literacy, and Electronics Training" in R. F. Dillion and J. W. Pellegrino (Eds.) *Instruction, Theoretical and Applied Perspectives*. New York: Praeger.

9. Kornbluth, H. and R. T. Greene (1989). "Learning, Empowerment, and Participative Work Process" in H. Leymann and H. Kornbluth (Eds.) *Socialization and Learning and Work*, pp. 256-74. Aldershot: Avebury.

10. Volpert, W. (1989). "Work and Personality Development from the Viewpoint of the Action Regulation Theory" in H. Leymann and H. Kornbluth (Eds.) *Socialization and Learning and Work*. Aldershot: Avebury.

11. Rubenson, K. (1989). "The Sociology of Adult Education" in S. B. Merriam and P. M. Cunningham (Eds.) *Handbook of Adult and Continuing Education*, pp. 51-69. San Francisco: Jossey-Bass. Rubenson, K. and G. Schutze (1992). *Learning At and Through the Workplace — A Review of Participation and Adult Learning Theory*. Vancouver: Department of Education, University of British Columbia.

12. Mezirow, Jack (1991). *Transformative Dimension of Adult Learning*. San Francisco: Jossey-Boss.

13. Marsick, V. J. (1988a). "Learning in the Workplace: The Case for Reflectivity and Critical Reflectivity." *Adult Education Quarterly 38*(4), 187-98. Marsick, V. J. (1988b). *Enhancing Staff Development in Diverse Settings*. San Francisco: Jossey-Bass.

14. Marsick, V. J. (1988a). "Learning in the Workplace."

15. Zacharakis-Jutz and F. M. Shied (1993). "Workers' Education, Social Construction, and Adult Education." *Adult Education Quarterly, 43*(2), pp. 101-09.

16. Fryer, B. (1990). "The Challenge to Working-Class Education" in B. Simon (Ed.) *The Search for Enlightenment*, pp. 276-319. London: Lawrence and Wishart.

17. Fryer, B. (1990). "The Challenge to Working-Class Education," p. 311.

18. Deutsch, S. (1989). "Worker Learning in the Context of Changing Technology and Work Environment" in Leymann and Kornbluth (Eds.) *Socialization and Learning at Work*, pp. 237-55. Vermont: Gower.

19.   Rubenson, K. and G. Schutze (1992). *Learning At and Through the Workplace — A Review of Participation and Adult Learning Theory*. Vancouver: University of British Columbia. Rubenson, K. (1989). "The Sociology of Adult Education" in S. B. Merriam and P. M. Cunningham (Eds.) *Handbook of Adult and Continuing Education*, pp. 51-69. San Francisco: Jossey-Bass.

20.   Ravid, G. (1987). "Self-Directed Learning in industry" in V. Marsick (Ed.) *Learning in the Workplace*, pp. 101-18. New York: Croom Helm.

21.   Kornbluth, H. and R. T. Greene (1989). "Learning, Empowerment, and Participative Work Process" in H. Leymann and H. Kornbluth (Eds.) *Socialization and Learning and Work*, pp. 256-74. Aldershot: Avebury.

22.   Deutsch, S. (1989). "Worker Learning in the Context of Changing Technology and Work Environment."

CHAPTER THREE

EMPLOYEES RETRAINING SCHEME: ORIGIN AND EVOLUTION

Introduction

In order to understand the economic environment into which the Employees Retraining Scheme (ERS) fits, it is useful to look, first, at the overall context of Hong Kong's recent economy. As one of the four Asian New Industrializing Countries (NICs), Hong Kong has had very remarkable export-led economic success in the last quarter century. The export sector has experienced very high growth during the last three decades and accounts for a large share of the gross domestic product. In 1983-84, exports accounted for close to 104 percent of its respective Gross Domestic Product (GDP), with re-exports constituting over 50 percent of the whole. In 1990, exports constituted 135 percent of its GDP.[1] Since 1979, Hong Kong has based its export strategy on the diversification of key manufacturing activities as well as on rapidly growing tertiary services.[2]

Except for infrastructure and education, Hong Kong has adopted non-interventionist economic policies, and these are considered to be the key of its success.[3] Many economists have argued that Hong Kong represents a classic example of economic non-interventionism. Their interpretation is, in large measure, influenced by the perception of the government. It has prided itself on the merits of non-interventionism and argued that the role of the government is to facilitate industrial and trade activities within the framework of a free market. Thus, it neither protects nor subsidizes manufacturers.[4]

Similarly, the government has been largely uninvolved in the promotion of workers' education and retraining. For a long time, Hong Kong has been the only one of the four "Asian Tigers" (Singapore, Taiwan, and South Korea) which has a system in which the individual himself takes primary responsibility for a good part of his retraining and advanced training. This lack of attention given to workers' retraining in Hong Kong might be surprising since there is often a positive relationship between training and productive potentials of workers.[5] Moreover, it is highly probable that Hong Kong workers, like the workers of Singapore, are undertrained at almost all levels in regard to both their general and technical educations.[6]

Perhaps for these reasons, in 1992 the government broke its long tradition of economic non-intervention and became active in workers' retraining by establishing the ERS. This scheme addressed older workers displaced by economic restructuring, and reoriented them to new jobs or provided training for new skills through specially devised programs. A 1995 study found that some 7,000 people have completed retraining and found jobs through this scheme. The government optimistically predicts that the scheme will very likely reach its yearly target of 10,000 people at the end of the year.[7]

Given the laissez-faire tradition, why is there any government intervention in labor retraining? This book will examine and critique the accuracy of the interpretation given by laissez-faire economists. It is argued by the authors that, contrary to the stated policy, the conception of a minimal state is not at all feasible on all occasions. Rather, the government does intervene in selected areas at important times for its own interests. As in any other society, in Hong Kong political and social needs may take precedent over economic philosophy in public policy-making. The authors believe the government's current involvement constitutes one of these exceptional occasions.

To show this, let us first explore the forces which shape the government's labor policy in training and discuss the objectives and implementation of the new retraining policy. Specifically, it is useful to identify the socio-political and economic factors which account for Hong Kong's adoption of a workers' retraining program, particularly as regards the development experiences of Hong Kong relating to education, employment, and training.

Hong Kong's Economic History — Vocational Training

Hong Kong has been a British colony since 1842. It was acquired by the British after their victory in a Sino-British war (the First Opium War). The major purpose of that war was to force China to open up its ports to foreign trade, and become a trading center, providing an entry-point to China. Hence, the primary aim of the colonial government was to protect and sustain the profit and privileges of the British merchants. This policy has remained largely unchanged, though it was modified by the trend of decolonization in the world politics and rapid economic development in Hong Kong after the Second World War. After the United Nations imposed a boycott on trade with China in early 1950s because of the Korean War, Hong Kong temporarily lost its entrepot trade but it rapidly developed a light manufacturing base and became a major exporter of textiles, garments, plastics and electronic products. Currently, in addition to its entrepot trade and manufacturing industries, it is an important financial, banking, and communications center in the region. It is considered as the third largest financial center in the world.[8]

Throughout the period of British rule, the philosophy of laissez-faire capitalism has been consistently upheld, including low tax rates, minimal customs duties, limited public spending, and ease of capital movement. In addition, the government has followed a long-standing policy of non-intervention in the labor market. Jointly, these approaches have ensured a low tax and cheap labor environment for capitalist investments.

However, although labor retraining had received little attention from the government prior to 1991, workers' education and training had not been totally neglected. Since the early 1970s, social workers and union organizers, with the conviction that workers, as a group, are neglected, have arranged some broad-based labor education courses for industrial workers.[9] These include: skills-training course, English course, labor law classes, civic and moral education, and various consciousness-raising courses. Part of the training needs of industrial workers (career guidance, pre-vocational training, and general labor education) is met by various adult education agencies in the colony. Some of these are "retrieval education," or education for those adults who did not have the opportunity of getting primary and/or secondary education.[10]

In the late 1970s, the government began to realize the need for in-service training because private firms were not actively involved in the training of individuals. Public-sector training centers were set up in order to implement training to better adjust supply and demand in the labor market. The basic approach was a liberal one in that these centers were open to any training needs of the firms but they were neither induced nor constrained to use them. Similarly, individuals were free to join these courses although incentives to undertake training were quite limited.[11]

This somewhat haphazard arrangement was unusual, given that overall, Hong Kong stands out in investment in educational infrastructures when compared with other developing countries. It has, and continues to develop, a substantial system of general education which is given high priority in the government budget. The government has realized the need of vocational training as back-up for its export-led industrialization. Vocational training needs are provided through a system of technical education and industrial training which helps school-leavers prepare for specific careers. Publicly-funded technical education is provided through the Vocational Training Council which operates two technical colleges and seven technical institutes.[12] The establishment of the Vocational Training Council was a significant step forward in skills training or worker training. It was set up in 1982 and financed entirely by the government. Its 24 industrial training centers today provide basic training and skills upgrading for industrial craftsmen and technicians, and for clerical and supervisory personnel in the service sector. All 24 centers offer courses on a part-time, evening and day-release basis so that they are open to in-service training. Besides these centers, the Vocational Training Council is responsible for initiating, developing, and running training activities for specialized or skilled labor and for technicians and technologists needed for industry.[13] In spite of this provision, it has to be noted, however, that government spending in vocational and industrial training is rather small compared with spending for general education.

In essence, the promotion of in-service training has been limited to introducing a vocational training infrastructure or mobilizing universities and technical institutes for ongoing training. Students have been either school leavers or those currently employed. By contrast, large-scale government involvement in the retraining of displaced workers has not been usual until recently. For a long time, the Labour Department has only provided very limited service (job information and referral service) for the unemployed. This has changed with the coming of the ERS.

Employees Retraining Scheme: Objectives and Structure

The introduction of the retraining scheme took place against a background of impressive economic growth, as the Hong Kong economy continued to grow steadily throughout the 1980s. It was still an important export-oriented economy. The growth rate in real terms of the gross domestic product was 2.8 percent in 1989, 3.0 percent in 1990 and 3.9 percent in 1991. Essential to its economic growth, the workforce in Hong

Kong was about 2.8 million (1991 figures), of whom 63 percent were male and 37 percent female. Of this workforce, 26.5 percent were engaged in wholesale and retail trades, restaurants and hotels, 9.7 percent in transport, storage and communications, 8.3 percent in construction, 8.4 percent in financing, insurance, real estate and business services, and 26.4 percent in manufacturing. Unemployment in 1991 was about 2.1 percent and underemployment 1.5 percent.[14]

As a result of economic activities continuing at a relatively high level, the labor market remained very tight. The government in fact used to claim that there was such insignificant unemployment in the colony that it had no obligation to provide retraining or assistance to workers. However, there had been increasing pressure upon the government to change its role in human resource policy in the early 1990s. A look at the main provisions of the scheme is given here.

The Employees Retraining Ordinance was first proclaimed in October 1992 to establish the Employees Retraining Board (ERB) and the Employees Retraining Fund (ERF). Today, the Board consists of 17 members, all appointed by the Hong Kong Governor. Its main functions are:

1. To administer the ERF, receiving all the levies payable by employers who employ imported workers.

2. To be responsible for the provisions, administration, and availability of retraining courses.

3. To identify sections of industry that require trained employees.

4. To liaise with and engage the services of training bodies.

The objectives of the Scheme, as stated by Dr. Samuel Wong, the former Chairman of the ERB, are:

> The short-term objective of ERS is to help local workers facing difficulties to find new jobs soon. The medium-term goal is to offer basic training courses, such as language training courses, to increase retrainees' skills so that they may return to the labor market on their own. The long term goal is to upgrade skills, increase the productivity of local workers and support the development of the local economy in the direction of high value added products.
>
>   (Legislative Council, May 1993)[15]

In practice, the Board decides what "skills" are required in the labor market and funds some training institutes to design and organize the relevant courses. Information on skills shortages are provided by other government departments such as the Labour Department or Census and Statistics. As of September of 1992, the statistics of employment vacancies indicated that manpower was most needed in the clothing industry, with 11,381 posts vacant in clothing manufacturing. It was followed by 7,384 vacancies in wholesale and retail, and 5,400 in catering. For the same period, the government received applications for importing 23,800 workers in the catering industry, 17,636 in clothing manufacturing and 12,018 in wholesales and retails from local employers.

After determining which sectors have surplus workers and which require retrained workers, the ERB sponsors courses organized by existing non-governmental agencies to equip eligible workers with the appropriate skills. The course design and delivery itself are the responsibility of the training bodies. In late 1994, there were about 12 publicly-funded education institutes or non-profit making organizations which submitted proposals and budgets to "sell" their courses to the ERB. These training bodies have various backgrounds and expertise which determine what types of courses they propose and in what format. Most courses funded by the Board are for skills training.

Initially, the Board was granted an advance of HK$300 million (US$38 million) by the government to start the project. In addition to this reserve fund, a provisional fund was set up by a levy imposed on employers importing workers from outside of Hong Kong at the rate of HK$400 (US$50) per worker per month. From these reserves, workers undergoing training have been entitled to a training allowance equal to half of the average median wage of an operative in the manufacturing sector. In order to join the retraining program, the workers must meet the following criteria:

1. The applicant must be a Hong Kong permanent resident.

2. Workers have to have been with the same employer/industry for at least two years and have lost or be about to lose their jobs because their plants or businesses have closed down or moved, their position or shifts have been abolished or not enough work has been made available for them to do.

3. Workers must have the necessary aptitude, education, and physique required by the relevant retraining programs.

4. Priority is given to workers aged above 30 but below 55 who are currently unemployed or underemployed. (Since 1995, housewives have also been able to join the scheme.)

To qualify for a retraining allowance, the trainees must attend a retraining program organized by a training institution or agency recognized by the ERB. Further, they must satisfy the attendance requirements and have good attendance records. They have had to register with the Local Employment Service for employment assistance but no suitable employment could be found.

To summarize, the manifest objectives of the retraining scheme are to provide retraining opportunities and a job referral system to help displaced workers find new jobs and to alleviate the problem of acute labor shortages in some sectors of the economy. It also enables housewives to re-enter the job market. However, the latent motives are much more complex and they affect how the retraining program works in practice.

Factors Contributing to the ERS

A closer scrutiny of the forces which shape this policy is necessary before any evaluation could be made. Probably such forces would affect or even determine how the training program would be configured.

(A) Economic Transition: Decline of Manufacturing Industry

Manufacturing and export have been the main sources of economic growth in Hong Kong since the 1950s. However, there has been a continuous decline in the size of the industrial employment in the manufacturing sector and a concomitant shift of workers from secondary to the tertiary sector since the late 1970s. The sectoral shift can be seen in terms of share of GDP. The relative contribution of the manufacturing sector to the GDP declined from 31 percent in 1970 to 24 percent in 1980 and again to 16 percent in 1991.

At the same time, the contribution of the tertiary service sector (comprising wholesale, retail and trades, restaurant and hotels, community and personal services, and other business services) increased from 63 percent in 1980 to 74 percent in 1991. With regard to employment, the most notable change since the early 1970s is that, whereas the manufacturing sector still takes up a significant proportion of the workforce, its share has been on a continuous decline from 47 percent in 1981 to 28 percent in 1991. On the other hand, the share of the tertiary service sector in total employment increased from 41 percent in 1971 to 47 percent in 1981, and to 63 percent in 1991.[16] The "Manpower Outlook in the 1990s" issued by the Education and Manpower Branch of the government forecast correctly that the overall manpower growth would be 7.7 percent per annum for all occupations for the period 1990-91. However, the majority was for the service sector, and there was a drop of some 86,000 persons (11 percent) in employment in the manufacturing sector for the same period. The pattern of growth between 1996 and 2001 is expected to be quite similar. One major increase will be the number of professional, technical, and managerial workers which will grow by some 12 percent.

There are many factors behind the economic sectoral shift such as the persistent growth of tourism, strong recovery in entrepot trade with China, fierce competition in trade with rapidly developing countries in the region, and the trend of continued relocation of manufacturing plants from Hong Kong to China since the late 1980s. All of these have significant implications for the labor market, since a large number of manufacturing workers are out of work. For example, the number of unemployed rose from 50,300 in 1991 to 54,600 in 1992, the underemployed from 44,500 to 58,300 over the same period. The majority of these employees were middle-aged, semi-skilled or non-skilled blue-collar workers. By one count, by late 1995, in manufacturing alone, the economic transition had resulted in a total loss of 600,000 factory jobs since the mid-1980s. Before the introduction of the ERS, these unemployed had to seek other jobs without government grants, tax incentives or assistance of any kind. As noted by Mr. T. S. Chow, the Executive Director of the Employees Retraining Board, these workers

> having made significant contributions towards the growth of Hong Kong in their early working lives, . . . are facing hard times. We are in sympathy with them, and we are here to lend a hand.

Thus the ERS was launched to provide career reorientation to the displaced workers.

However, it is doubtful that the retraining scheme was founded solely on such humane grounds. Historically, the Hong Kong colonial state has not played a role in facilitating the development of particular industries or of monitoring industrial restructuring.[17] A more plausible explanation lies in the policy linkages to changes in the political structure and to market failures.

(B) The Limitations of the Labor Market

It has been fashionable to attribute government intervention in industrial restructuring to the failure of markets. Obviously, there are many difficulties with an approach which relies solely on market and individual initiatives. This is well exemplified in the area of in-service training.

Experience from in-service training has shown that insufficient support from the government has given rise to numerous problems. The first difficulty is the lack of motivation with respect to in-service training among semi- or unskilled workers on account of the lack of opportunities for promotion or wage increase after training. The second difficulty is the labor market's failure to recognize the skills acquired in in-service training via certification. The third has to do with choosing from among the huge amounts of information available on training. This information is insufficient for making well-informed decisions at the individual or collective level.[18]

The government is not unaware of these problems which could reduce opportunities for workers' training. However, the official policy of voluntarism is so steadfastly upheld that retraining (implying more in-depth intervention) would be the last policy option.

In actuality, there are some economic hypotheses which support government intervention in workers' training. The key economic argument which underpins the shortfall in training provision can be explicable in terms of market failure.[19] There are three main forms of market failure which explain why the market might under-provide for training. First, individuals may be deterred from training because the capital market is imperfect. In other words, individual workers cannot finance the training which they would otherwise be willing to undertake. Second, there is the problem of "poaching" — firms fail to train because they fear that non-training firms will lure their trained workers away. Third, employment contracts may restrict employers and workers from achieving an efficient outcome. This means that an efficient outcome cannot be obtained without some re-contracting to reflect the unanticipated changes in the value of human capital.

Obviously, some of these economic propositions are applicable to Hong Kong. There is increasing evidence that workers in Hong Kong cannot afford to finance training, particularly those workers who are laid off. A number of factors are limiting training opportunities, the most important being the inertia of management. Businesses are especially short-sighted in that they want to reap profits as soon as practicable. They are also wary of the political changes that might take place after the 1997 hand-over of the colony to China. Training is thus not given much weight. Further, labor mobility is very high in Hong Kong. Because of this, firms run the risk of not benefitting from the training investments they make, and consequently, they tend to restrict those investments.

It might be argued that because market mechanisms had failed in the past, some form of institutional framework is necessary for the functions that the market cannot perform. This is seen in the case of Vocational Training Council, which was set up to coordinate in-service training and provide ongoing and basic training. Not surprisingly, when unemployment worsens and affects many more workers and when those workers are not school-leavers, the need for a second institutional framework to do the retraining of workers is obvious.

On the other hand, the government has not had adequate warning of rapid economic transitions and their possible repercussions on employment prospects. Although the government had continued to invest heavily in general education, there were simply insufficient opportunities for displaced workers to receive retraining before 1992. Further, workers, especially the older ones, had not realized the urgency of upgrading their skills before their present ones became outdated. The government never issued policy initiatives stating that upgrading skills to the levels of developed countries would be necessary to justify higher wages.

(C) Policy Linkages: General Labor Importation Policy

Despite the surplus of labor in the manufacturing sector, the problem of "labor shortages" started to hit Hong Kong in the late 1980s. As a result, employers lobbied for the massive import of semi-skilled and unskilled workers to alleviate the problem. In 1989, the government allowed the importation of 3,000 skilled workers on contracts not exceeding two years. Subsequently, 2,323 workers were admitted into Hong Kong working mostly in the construction and manufacturing sectors. Their employers were required to supply them with housing and to pay them wages not lower than the local levels. But there have been many claims that some workers are paid less than the levels specified in their contracts.

This has taken place amid a general tightening of the labor market in Hong Kong, which is attributable to a number of factors: low natural growth of the population, the leveling-off of the labor force participation rate, emigration of workers (who are fearful of the return of Hong Kong to Communist China in 1997), and sustained growth of the economy. Meanwhile, economic reform in China has resulted in the relocation of plants from Hong Kong to neighboring China because of cheaper labor costs.[20] The report, "A Ten Year Vision and Agenda for Hong Kong's Economy" issued by the Business and Professionals Federation of Hong

Kong in 1993 shows that approximately 75 percent of manufacturing companies now have plants in China. It is estimated that at least 50,000 workers were laid off from the manufacturing sector during 1993 and over 10,000 are unable to find new jobs.[21] The chance of these workers finding new employment is limited, due to their low education qualifications and lack of job skills other than those specific to their old trades. They are disadvantaged in competing with the imported laborers in the unskilled job market because the latter are usually younger and paid at lower wages.

A government plan to import 14,700 workers mostly from China, was much welcomed by the businessmen. But local union leaders were quick to condemn this move, claiming that a large number of imported workers would depress local wages and place undue pressure on social services.[22] They were assiduous in lobbying against the government and urging it to rescind the newly-introduced special scheme on imported labor. But the voices of employers prevailed in this case. The government decided to allow an annual recruitment of 25,000 foreign workers but insisted that permission to hire must be obtained from the government by the employers.

Many critics of these developments see a link between the introduction of the workers' retraining scheme and the government's "imported labor policy." Labor relations analysts point out that the government has abandoned the long-standing policy of non-intervention because it wants to make the importation of labor more palatable to local workers and unions and to address the problem of rising unemployment among some declining industries, as for example, electronics and manufacturing.[23] In short, the policy impetus of the retraining scheme comes from the implementation and ramifications of the preceding policy on labor supply. It also represents a compromise, a trade-off, and a balance of forces between business and labor groups.

(D) A Corporatist Government and Increased Labor Power

Politically, the British have imposed on Hong Kong a constitutional framework which has remained largely unchanged since its inception. The British government has complete executive and legislative authority over Hong Kong. The governor, who has ultimate power within the territory, is appointed by the Queen. He makes all local policies and is accountable only to the British government. There is a legislative council in the colony which plays an advisory role. Until 1986, all the members of the legislative council were appointed by the governor. Therefore, for a long time, businessmen and industrialists have been "over-represented" in the legislature while trade unions and labor groups have been peripheral and considered as politically dangerous to the development of the economy. The alliance between business interests and the colonial government thus, is quite overt. Legislation for the protection of labor has been belated and incomprehensive. The lack of interest on the part of government in labor matters is further fueled by the weak labor movement in the colony.

This scenario of weak labor representation has changed recently. In 1984, the Sino-British Joint Declaration on the Future of Hong Kong was initialed in Beijing. Through this accord, the British government agreed to return the colony to the Chinese government in 1997. It has become clear that China would resume the exercise of sovereignty over Hong Kong and its administration in 1997. Given a prevalent distrust of the Communist rule, the people of Hong Kong began to face the challenge of maintaining the territory's stability and prosperity. Because of this impending change-over, the British began to introduce changes in government by allowing 24 elected members to join the legislature, although another 22 members were still appointed by the governor. Twelve of the elected members came from the functional constituencies (including professional bodies and business groups) and two of the seats in the functional constituencies were elected by the registered employee trade unions. Although the new structure has been labeled as "corporatist" by some academics, it is a break form the past where labor interests were more often than not disregarded.[24] In the context of Hong Kong, this corporatism means a pattern of interest intermediation and a mode of policy formation in which formally designated interest associations are incorporated within the processes of decision-making and implementation of policies.

Nevertheless, there has been no meaningful attempt to change the power pattern; power remains concentrated in a small group of elites — top civil servants, businessmen and professional elites. The limited innovations are the institutionalized system of interest intermediation in which labor-community groups are represented and the government attempts to strengthen the professional elites as allies of the business leaders in ruling Hong Kong. However, the two trade union representatives in the legislature are able to wield some influence over government labor policy. This is not surprising, as one representative comes from a pro-Beijing trade union and the government cannot afford to ignore the opinions of the Beijing government. Further, local labor groups have rallied behind the elected representatives in a number of labor issues and have successfully obtained concessions from the government. With the introduction of direct elections in 1991 and 1995 and a gradual formal democratization in the years to come, the labor-community groups have a louder voice in policy-making. In this respect, the implementation of the new retraining program can be interpreted as one example where the government tries to accommodate the interests of labor and capitalists. In fact, the capitalists' interests are still enhanced by the retraining program since they can get skillful workers from the existing pool of retrainees while the government is still paying for the training costs.

(E) New International Division of Labor

The thesis of "new international division of labor" can throw more light on the evolution of ERS. International division of labor is a way of increasing production, reducing dependency on skilled labor and habituating a recalcitrant workforce to the rhythm of mechanized work.[25] The distinctive feature of the present form of international division of labor is the relocation of certain industries or segments of industries to the peripheral countries. That is to say, multinational companies have begun to relocate industrial production from high-wage sites in wealthier nations to low-wage sites in poor countries.[26] Equally important is the phenomenon of abundant use of female labor.[27]

International division of labor represents a new type of capital penetration of underdeveloped countries which can be traced back to the 1960s. Then, transnational enterprises started operations in certain countries for the manufacture of goods for export in order to benefit from the particularly favorable conditions offered by the existence of highly productive low-cost labor. As Henderson and Castells[28] succinctly put it, there is an increasing internationalization of the economy, taking advantage of the most favorable locations for production, management, and control of the markets, while maintaining an interconnected world-wide system. In these developing countries, capital displays a tendency to hire very selectively only those workers whom it considers most "efficient." After literally exhausting their labor power, they are displaced by new workers.

This process explains massive outflow of capital from Hong Kong to China and other Asian countries like Vietnam and Indonesia in order to take advantage of the low labor costs there. This has taken place on a large scale ever since the mid-1980s, when many factories or firms in the colony were closed down and relocated to neighboring areas of mainland China, e.g., Guangdong Province, which is a highly controlled society. In Hong Kong, the comparative advantage brought by imported cheap labor has now disappeared. Comparatively, workers in China are cheap and highly disciplined and labor unrest is extremely rare. Thus, China provides excellent preconditions for investments of transnational companies from all countries.

Since the adoption of "open door" policies by China in late 1978, Hong Kong's economic relations with China have undergone very rapid changes. As far as trade is concerned, the two are each other's major trading partners.[29] As for investment, Hong Kong has always been a convenient gateway to China for businesses, both local and international. Hong Kong is the most important source of external investment in China, accounting for about two-thirds of the total in 1994. Hong Kong's direct investment in China has been concentrated in light manufacturing industries and investments in hotels and tourist-related facilities. More recently, investment in property and infrastructure has been increasing. It has been estimated that in Guangdong Province, more than three million people are working for Hong Kong companies, either through joint ventures or in tasks commissioned by Hong Kong firms.[30] At present, there are about 25,000 factories in Guangdong manufacturing products for Hong Kong businessmen. More than 80 percent of the labor-intensive industries run by Hong Kong businessmen have moved to Guangdong. Owing to relatively low land and labor costs in China, this "manufacturing emigration" from Hong Kong to Guangdong contributes to the economic growth of Hong Kong,[31] as well as to the unemployment of Hong Kong residents.

Another aspect of the internationalization of labor concerns women. Today, more and more women (who are mostly peasants) in China are hired in the new manufacturing factories owned by Hong Kong and transnational businesses. This internationalization of labor took root in Communist China after it embarked on a market strategy of development in the 1980s. Cohen[32] rightly observes that the success of export-oriented manufacturing has been predicated on the use of cheap, largely non-unionized, young, female workers who make up 70 to 80 percent of the world's labor force in the processing zones of the Third World. According to the Guangdong's Women's Association, in 1995 women made up 46 percent of the province's workforce.[33] The entry of this significant group of women from China to the manufacturing labor force attests to this contention.

On the other hand, "extensive pauperization" strikes the manufacturing workers (mostly women) in Hong Kong who are displaced when the plants are closed down and moved to China. They now have more and more difficulties in seeking alternative jobs. They could easily become a source of discontent if the government does not do something for them.

Problems of Employees Retraining Scheme

Since its inception, the ERS has encountered a number of problems. They concern its financing, programming, and long-term planning. In spite of these, the ERS is increasingly conceived as a solution to the problem of increasing unemployment in the colony.

(1) Rising Unemployment

While Hong Kong has seen periods of near full employment (particularly from 1990 to 1994), many workers have also faced difficulties with such basic needs as housing, unemployment benefits, pensions, and welfare provision for old age. However, this situation has changed rapidly since early 1995. There are numerous signs of a slowing down of activity. Unemployment worsened quickly from 2.0 percent in 1994 to 3.6 percent in early 1996. Unemployment rate at that time was at an 11-year high. Hardest hit were the manufacturing and construction sectors. A recent study by the Organization for Economic Co-operation and Development noted that Hong Kong has been hit by a weakening of growth in China and an adverse impact of falling domestic property and asset prices.[34]

Other information which is available indicates that people are getting pessimistic about the future. Two recent surveys showed that Hong Kong manufacturers were uncertain about prospects in the next two years. The 1995 survey of manufacturers, which was conducted by the government, revealed that more than three quarters of the 2,081 companies surveyed thought their business prospects were either weak or uncertain. Looking forward to 1997, respondents who believed their future was uncertain or weak rose to 87 percent. A second survey of foreign investment in Hong Kong revealed that nearly 70 percent of foreign firms believed their prospects would be more uncertain or weaker in 1997 than they were at the time of the survey. As a consequence, about 19 percent of manufacturers intended to phase out their production in Hong Kong.[35]

Among workers, the same mood prevails. A recent survey showed that more workers were worried about being sacked than ever before.[36] One-third of the 1,030 respondents, aged between 15 and 64, were worried they might lose jobs soon. This compared with a figure of 19 percent in a similar survey the previous quarter. Blue-collar workers aged about 40 with little education or low incomes emerged as the most anxious group.

Higher unemployment and uncertain political prospects have made both government and trade unions revise their expectations of the ERS. They now expect this program to be an effective mechanism of helping unemployed workers find new employment. New significance is now attached to this program. However, it is doubtful if this program, which was originally small-scale, transitory, and unplanned, can be adjusted to meet the new demands. A look at its shaky financial base would reveal the limits of this program.

(2) Finance

Since its establishment, a critical issue which the ERS faces is financing. The financial capability of the ERB is getting more precarious. As it stands, it lacks a long-term alternative source of funding. Currently, the ERB is funded by the employers of 50,000 foreign workers under the general and airport labor importation schemes, which pay HK$400 (US$50) for each person they take on. This link between imported labor and ERB's income base means extra vulnerability if imported workers are not allowed. Thus, as the ERB looks forward to the completion of Hong Kong's new airport in 1998 and the consequential reduction in the number of imported workers, they fear being too hard-up to retrain the unemployed. This threat is real, since the recurrent spending of the ERB exceeded their annual income in 1995. The executive director of the board said the problem is not imminent since the board has sufficient funding for at least the next two years. Nevertheless, it is imperative that the board looks for a long-term alternative source of income.[37]

Rising unemployment, also, is a double-edged sword. As unemployment continues to soar, the need for retraining will get stronger because there are increasing numbers of unemployed workers. Paradoxically, this would also put the program in jeopardy because the recent sharp rise in unemployment has sparked new discontent and anger among trade unionists, who see the importation of labor policy as the primary culprit which robs them of their jobs. In response to this, the government argues that there is no connection between unemployment and importation of labor.

All along, the financial resources for the ERB were designed to be secure only if the importation of labor policy were firmly in place. In face of high unemployment (3.6 percent in late 1995, the highest in 11 years), the Hong Kong government was under strong pressure to scrap its labor importation policy. In mid-1995, Governor Patten first admitted that there was some connection between rising unemployment and importation of foreign workers. A freeze of the importation of labor policy was imposed and this quickly reduced the income of the ERB from its levy.

Then, in late 1995, all political parties in the Legislative Council (except the Liberal Party which has always championed the wishes of business) called for an end to the importation of labor scheme. The Liberal Party argued that big companies and small businesses would find it hard to employ qualified workers if this proposal was adopted. Thus, it urged the government not to give more away to soothe the labor movement.[38] However, the government was willing to grant some concessions to trade unions. The final proposal represented a compromise of employers and employees' interest: the number of imported workers would be reduced but a ceiling would not be set. Worsening employment prospects and the strong opposition from trade unions to imported laborer policy are two factors which the government cannot afford not to heed. The proposal finally got through the Legislative Council in early 1996. The Legislature decided that the General Labour Importation Scheme would be replaced by a Supplementary Labour Scheme which provided for a limited number of imported workers. This, of course, would further reduce the income available from levies. Because of the worsening financial situation, the government announced in its 1996-97 budget that another HK$300 million (US$38 million) be injected into the ERB's reserves.[39]

(3) Programming and Delivery

Another corollary of the rise in unemployment is that stronger criticisms of the retraining scheme are now heard. In other words, the whole program is now put under very strict scrutiny. In addition to criticizing its weak financial base, trade union leaders have argued that the retraining scheme lacks long-term planning and is overly concerned with statistics. They claim that it lacks a clear vision because it is basically a stop-gap measure. The ERB has very few ideas as to where the whole program is heading. There is a distinct lack of co-ordination between industrial training policy and overall economic policy.

Increasingly, the scheme has come under attack for its inability to deal with abuses of the program. Some people just enroll in the part-time courses in order to get the allowance and have no desire to receive training nor look for jobs. Statistics of the number of people in retraining are also questioned by some critics since they claim that the ERB is over-zealous with figures in order to legitimize its existence.

Most damaging is the criticism as to the relevance of retraining courses. Some adult education academics say that the program has failed to prepare middle-aged workers for new employment. Mr. Y. C. Tam, the new Chairman of the ERB, accepted this criticism but claimed this was reasonable, citing some garment workers who took intensive computer courses offered by the ERB. He noted that:

> Most of them have been working in garment factories for decades. And now you want to train them to be qualified computer operators in three weeks. It is not possible at all.[40]

Critics also argue that the latent goal which underlies the whole ERS program is that the government only wants low or minimum skill standards rather than high quality training. They claim this policy is an extension of the underlying laissez-faire philosophy of the government — responsibility of training lies with individuals rather than government or the private sector. It is worth repeating that many firms in Hong Kong are not active in the training of their workers.

Conclusion

The advent of the ERS is a signal that the government intervention in labor retraining is now called for. However, this program does not mean the end of laissez-faire policy. Essentially, it reveals that the government has used a reactive approach in the retraining of workers. The ERS is problem-solving in nature, and seeks to address only the growing problem of unemployment, rather than improve the productivity of the labor force. From the perspective of government, the ERS represents a compromise of labor and business interests and provides a bureaucratic cushion against mounting criticisms of the importation of labor policy. The irony is that, as unemployment soars, the program is now looked upon as a panacea to unemployment. It is highly doubtful whether this retraining program, without many adjustments and much hard thinking, could ever meet this new challenge.

◆   ◆   ◆

NOTES

1.   Krueger, Anne (1995). "East Asian Experience and the Endogenous Growth Theory" in Takatoshi Ito and Anne Krueger (Eds.) *Growth Theories in Light of the East Asian Experience*, pp. 9-36. Chicago: University of Chicago Press.

2.   Salome, Bernard and Jacques Charmes (1988). *In-Service Training: Five Asian Experiences*. Washington, D.C.: OECD.

3.   Krueger, Anne (1995). "East Asian Experience and the Endogenous Growth Theory," p. 9-10.

4.   Hong Kong Government (1996). *Hong Kong Annual Report 1996*. Hong Kong: Government Printer. The government has consistently expressed this view on various occasions and in official publications. One latest occasion was the Governor's final policy address in early October, 1996.

5.   Tang, Kwong-leung and Jacqueline Tak-york Cheung (1996). "Models of Workplace Training in North America: A Review." *International Journal of Lifelong Education*, 15(4), July-August, 1996, pp. 256-65.

6.   Jacqueline Tak-york Cheung (1994). *Models of Workplace Learning*. Unpublished Master of Education Thesis. Vancouver: University of British Columbia.

7.   *Hong Kong Economic Journal*, December 27, 1995.

8.   Kurian, G. T. (1992). *Encyclopedia of the Third World*. New York: Facts on File.

9.   Tang, Kwong-leung et al (1983). *Social Work for Industrial Workers*. Hong Kong: Hong Kong Social Workers' General Union.

10.   Dalglish, C. (1984). *Adult Education in Hong Kong*. Paper presented in National Institute of Continuing Education.

11.   Salome and Charmes, 1988, Chapter 1.

12.   Hong Kong Government (1994). *Hong Kong Annual Report 1994*. Hong Kong: Government Printer.

13.   Salome and Charmes, 1988, Chapters 2-4.

14. Hong Kong Government (1992). *Annual Budget Speech.* Hong Kong: Government Printer.

15. Hong Kong Legislative Council (1993). *Legislative Council Minutes.* May Sessions. Hong Kong: Legco.

16. Hong Kong Government (1992). *Annual Statistics.* Hong Kong: Government Printer.

17. Levin, David and Stephen Chiu (1995). "Dependent Capitalism, A Colonial State, and Marginal Unions: The Case of Hong Kong" in Stephen Frankel (Ed.) *Organized Labor in the Asia-Pacific Region: A Comparative Study of Trade Unionism in Nine Countries,* pp. 187-222. Ithaca, New York: ILR Press.

18. Salome and Charmes, 1988, Final Chapter.

19. Chapman, Paul (1993). *The Economics of Training.* London: Harvester Wheatsheaf.

20. Siu, K. F. and Y. F. Luk (1990). "The State of the Economy" in Richard Wong and Joseph Cheng (Eds.) *The Other Hong Kong Report 1990,* pp. 205-20. Hong Kong: Chinese University of Hong Kong Press.

21. Tso, Wendy (1993). "Training Scheme Gives New Hope to Unemployed." *Hong Kong Industrialist,* pp. 20-21, July 1993.

22. Ng, S. H. (1990). "Labour and Employment" in R. Wong and Joseph Cheng (Eds.) *The Other Hong Kong Report 1990,* pp. 267-96. Hong Kong: Chinese University of Hong Kong Press.

23. Chan William (1993). "Retraining the Unemployed in Hong Kong." *HKCER Letters.*

24. Scott, Ian (1989). *Political Change and the Crisis of Legitimacy of Hong Kong.* Hawaii: University of Hawaii Press.

25. Boyd, Rosalind E., Robin Cohen and Peter Gutkind (Eds.) (1987). *International Labour and the Third World.* Aldershot: Avebury. Henderson J. and R. Cohen (1982). "On the Reproduction of the Relations of Production" in Ray Forest et al (Eds.) *Social Theory and Urban Political Economy.* Aldershot: Gower. Frobel, Folker (1980). *New International Division of Labour: Structural Unemployment in Industrialized Countries an Industrialization in Developing Countries.* London: Cambridge University Press.

26.   Hill, Richard C. (1987). "Global Factory and Company Town: The Changing Division of Labour in the International Automobile Industrial" in J. Henderson and M. Castells (Eds.) *Global Restructuring and Territorial Development*, pp. 18-37. Newbury Park: Sage.

27.   Frankel, Stephen (Ed.) (1993). *Organized Labor in the Asian-Pacific Region*. Ithaca, New York: ILR Press. Jacqueline Tak-york Cheung (1994). *Models of Workplace Training*, Chapter 3.

28.   Jeffrey Henderson and Manuel Castells (Eds.) (1987). *Global Restructuring and Territorial Development*, pp. 18-37. Newbury Park: Sage.

29.   Hong Kong Government (1994). *Hong Kong Annual Report 1994*. Hong Kong: Government Printer.

30.   Ibid.

31.   Ng, Shek-hong (1994). "The Role of the Government in Human Resources Development: Retrospect and Prospect" in Benjamin Leung and Teresa Wong (Eds.) *25 Years of Social and Economic Development in Hong Kong*, pp. 458-88. Hong Kong: University of Hong Kong Press.

32.   Cohen, Robin (1987). "Theorizing International Labour" in R. E. Boyd et al (Eds.) *International Labour and the Third World: The Making of a New Working Class*, pp. 3-25. Aldershot: Gower.

33.   *Sing Tao Daily News*, January 5, 1996.

34.   *Sing Tao Daily News*, December 20, 1995.

35.   *Sing Tao Daily News*, December 21, 1995.

36.   *South China Morning Post*, October 22, 1995.

37.   *South China Morning Post*, May 25, 1995.

38.   *Sing Tao Daily News*, January 4, 1996.

39.   Hong Kong Government (1996). *Annual Budget Speech 1996*. Hong Kong: Government Printer.

40.   *South China Morning Post*, October 22, 1995.

CHAPTER FOUR

EMPLOYEES RETRAINING SCHEME:
MODEL OF TRAINING

Originally, the government proposed to conduct eight pilot retraining programs in mid-1992.[1] An analysis of these pilot courses shows an over-emphasis on specific skills to the neglect of general job training. The skills courses included: print finishing, sample making, in-line quality control inspection, garment fitting alteration, hotel housekeeping and cleaning services, basic retail sales techniques, preparation of production orders, and shipping and documentation for the clothing industry. As mentioned above, the courses were selected based on figures obtained from the Census and Statistics Department and from employer's applications for imported labor which indicated labor shortages in the market. More recently, the types of courses organized by the ERB have expanded (Table 4.1) to provide more variety to more workers. It is noteworthy that for some courses, the enrollment rate was nil or very low. The ERB was requested by members of the Legislative Council to find out why the response to some courses like waiter/waitress was so low, while statistics indicated that there was a shortage of workers in high-demand sectors as, for example, the catering industry.[2] There seemed to be a discrepancy between courses provided and demands in the market.

Table 4.1

TRAINING COURSES OF EMPLOYEES RETRAINING SCHEME
(November 1993 to January 1994)

Course Title	Class Size
Hotel Housekeeping Cleaning Services	15
Fast Food Attendant	15
Computerized Chinese Typesetting	15
Warehousing Operations	15
Mould and Tooling Craftsmen and Technicians Retraining Courses	20
Office Chinese Computer Application	25
Import and Export Document Operator	25
Chinese Bookkeeping Training	25
Introduction to Desktop Publishing	20
Practical English (Elementary and Advanced)	20
Evening Course in Retail Service	20
Office Assistant Training	20
Basic Clerical Training	25
Evening Vocational English	20
Buildings Caretaker	20
English for Waiter/Waitress	20
Housekeeper Service	20
Evening Introduction to Typing	20
Evening Office Mandarin	20
Half-day Pre-job Training on Office Practice for Housewives	20
Core Course on Job Search Skills	20

Source: Progress Report on the Employees Retraining Scheme,
        November 1993 (Submitted to the Legislative Council)

Program Development

A preliminary evaluation of the ERS was thus made by the Education and Manpower Committee of the Legislative Council in mid-1993 which subsequently made the following changes to the scheme:

1. Extend the scheme to cover homemakers.

2. Arrange evening courses and On-the-job Training Schemes (OTS) to suit the different needs of workers and substantially increase the retraining capacity. Approved employers can claim training allowances from the government for each eligible worker they hire without going through any prior screening by the government.

3. Gather information on the jobs which the workers obtain after the completion of retraining.

4. Consider extending services to the aged and disabled populations.

Such changes do not alter the nature and contents of the retraining scheme.

As of May, 1993 (after nine months of implementation), 604 trainees had completed courses of the Employees Retraining Scheme. The ERB claimed a high success rate of retraining and placement of graduated trainees. Of the 604 trainees, 292 (48 percent) did not require the job placement service of the Labour Department and 232 (38 percent) were in employment. The remaining 80 (13.2 percent) still required job referral services. However, as pointed out by spokespersons of a labor organization, there was no information on the post-training employment status of the trainees who did not use the government employment services. Hence, there was no clear evidence showing that the retraining program was effective in relocating the displaced workers. There were also criticisms that the number of trainees was too small and there was no study on their characteristics.

In response to these criticisms, the ERB managed to provide a simple profile of the 604 trainee graduates. It was found that some three-quarters of the trainees were female (72 percent), 62 percent were aged between 30 and 39 and 32 percent between 40 and 49, 75 percent had completed Grade 9 or below, and over half of them (58 percent) came from the clothing industry and other manufacturing industries. In other words, a majority of the participants were female, middle-aged, poorly educated, and from the declining manufacturing industries. This profile of the trainees has remained largely unchanged except that since the first year, a large number of housewives have been recruited into the training program (Table 4.2). Over the years, it was occasionally announced that the capacity of the scheme would be expanded to provide additional courses catering to more trainees. The next quarterly report (November, 1993) of the ERB indicated that an additional 1,581 workers had completed skills retraining. Again, about 931 (59 percent) of the trainees did not seek employment through the Labour Department, 455 (29 percent) took up employment and the remaining 195 (12 percent) were still looking for jobs. There were no statistics on whether the employed trainees did get jobs in which they could put into practice what they had learned. For an overview of the types of courses the ERB organized, see Table 4.1.

Table 4.2

WORKING EXPERIENCES OF TRAINEES
(September 13 to October 31, 1993)

Category	Number	Percent
Housewives	552	25
Manufacturing	479	22
Electronics	195	9
Food	139	6
Servicing and Cleaning	75	3
Textiles	70	3
Retailing	57	3
Miscellaneous	605	29
Total	2,172	100%

Source: Panel on Manpower Meeting,
        Hong Kong Legislative Council,
        October 12, 1993

Model of Training

Given the diverse courses under the scheme, it is impossible to examine each and every one. Instead, we would like to review the overall scheme using the following indicators as discussed in Chapter Two: objectives of training, focus of training, format of learning, participation of workers, construction of knowledge, and concept of management. It cannot be over-emphasized that whether the ERB tends to follow a behavioral or worker-centered approach does not automatically make it a "bad" or a "good" program. However, the identification of the underlying training model is crucial in an analysis of the strengths and weaknesses of the program and in working for improvement.

Objectives of Training

As noted, the main objectives as announced by the ERB are to help the displaced workers to find jobs and to enhance the productivity of the local labor force. It sounds quite humanistic and worker-centered. However, there seems to be another agenda of a political and social nature involved. As described by a Legislative Council member:

> In order to pacify Hong Kong's labour sector, who were unhappy with the General Scheme of Importation of Labour, the Government, in the middle of last year, put forth the Employee's Retraining Scheme (ERS). This was done in a hurry, before there had been time for careful planning. The results of the ERS have therefore been disappointing.
>
> (Legislative Council, May 1993, 3821)[3]

Not only the hastiness with which the ERS was set up is questionable, the sincerity and commitment of the government in workers' retraining are also challenged due to the inconsistency of its labor policy. There are inherent conflicts between the interests of the dislocated workers and the policy of imported labor. Most displaced workers, due to their low academic qualifications, have to look for other semi-skilled or unskilled jobs in the labor market. Yet the employers are filling up these jobs with cheap labor imported from neighboring countries. Even those who have taken courses from the ERS find some difficulties in competing with foreign laborers because of the low wages accepted by the latter group. As pointed out by Y. C. Tam, who represents perspectives of labor unions in the Legislative Council, this results in a "situation of large-scale importation of labour versus small-scale retraining, and planned importation of labour versus haphazard provision of retraining."[4]

Indeed, the whole retraining scheme has been questioned by some labor organizations as more of an expedient to uphold the interests of big business rather than a forward-looking plan to enhance workers' competitiveness in the job market. Most of the courses offered under the ERS, such as Fast Food Attendant, Buildings Caretaker, Housekeeper Service and others, aim at equipping dislocated workers with very simple skills or semi-skills, to take up low-paying jobs in other sectors of industry where mass cheap labor is needed. Since training is not an important criterion to enter those jobs, the trainees have to compete with school leavers, foreign workers and other unskilled laborers for the same positions. The ERB has been criticized for showing more interest in finding out the statistics of course enrollment than the post-training employment situations of the trainees. Nor have there been any efforts made to ensure that trainees are able to find relevant new jobs. Hence, the ERS gives the impression of a scheme to meet manpower needs of capitalists rather than cater to the needs of workers.

Focus of Training

As explained by Samuel Wong, first Chairman of ERB, there are four main categories of courses that are subsidized. They are:

1. Technical training courses which last between four and sixteen weeks.
2. Induction courses on job search which consist of vocational counseling and last for a week.
3. Evening courses of practical language training and computer operations.
4. Skill upgrading courses which are more suitable for technicians than for displaced workers.

(Legislative Council, 1993)[5]

Further analysis of the training courses and the training institutes indicates that ten out of the 12 training bodies provided courses on technical training, four provided the one-week induction course, four provided language and computer courses and only two provided skills upgrading courses. At all times, a great majority of the courses are very job-specific and skill-oriented. For instance, "Carpentry and Joinery" is one of the few day-time courses that last as long as 20 weeks. Its course description emphasizes training in setting door frames, locks, metal works, ceiling, wall and partition, cabinetry and closets. The course outline for a ten-week course of "Import and Export Document Operator" focuses on using the typewriter and word-processor, creating documents for shipping and customs, understanding specific terms in the clothing industry and managing the filing system. "Housekeeper Service" is one of the shortest full-time courses, and lasts only four weeks. It provides basic training in room cleaning, understanding of different types of carpet and cleaning methods, safety measures, decoration in hotel rooms and basic social conversations with clients in English and Mandarin.[6] Since most of the courses last for only one to two months, their focus could only be "designed for adults who wish to acquire a specific . . . . skill in a relatively short period to enable them to [find a new job"].[7]

Finally, again, the assessment of the effectiveness of individual courses depends more on the number of those enrolled and the number of learners completing the courses successfully than it does on workers finding new jobs. There has been no systematic effort to ensure that the trainees are able to get into and adjust to a new field.

Format of Training

As admitted by the Secretary for Education and Manpower in a Legislative Council Meeting (May, 1993), the ERS started with courses of specific skills training delivered in the form of traditional classroom teaching. In response to continuous criticisms of this, the ERB has tended to fund an increased number of courses organized by more training institutes to provide a greater variety of contents.

On the other hand, the ERB does not interfere in the delivery of training programs. Each institute provides courses according to its own tradition. Some of the training bodies, such as the Construction Industry Training Authority, have a background of providing an apprenticeship style training to young people. Other agencies, such as Caritas and the Y.W.C.A., are experienced in providing formal and informal education.

However, regardless of provider agency, the contents and formats of the ERS courses are limited by their duration and resources. The median length of full-time courses is eight weeks (based on courses organized in July-September, 1993). The training bodies are expected to equip the trainees with basic skills of brand new jobs within approximately two months' time. In short, it is a "one-time, quick fix" remedial approach to the unemployment problem. An example is the course of Basic Clerical Training, where great emphasis is placed on learning to operate different types of machines of communication, word-processing and file management. All of these are taught in the form of lectures and practice with simulated office environments.

Another factor related to the course format is the quality of instructors, particularly as regards their understanding of the learning needs, learning styles, and learning barriers of the dislocated workers. No extra training is deemed necessary for the instructors of the ERS courses. Also, agencies often hire part-time staff to provide ERS courses in addition to their regular educational programs. Usually the part-time staff are selected solely on the basis of their knowledge of specific job skills. Undoubtedly, the focus of these instructors is purely job-specific. It is questionable whether the training therefore helps trainees to adjust to ongoing changes in the job markets. As things stand now, they may have to learn about another trade if there is further restructuring of the economy.

Some exceptions to the above are the orientation courses on Job Search Skills, skill upgrading courses, and the On-the-Job Training (OTJ) program. The one-week job search course itself focuses on job interview techniques. Great emphasis is placed on teaching the trainees how to sell themselves to human resource managers. Due to the intended vocational counseling elements in the course, the ERB does provide funding for the training of job search instructors. The training is organized in the form of four workshops, each lasting about three hours. The instructors are sponsored to participate on a voluntary basis. However, the effectiveness of this instructor-training program is unclear because it is not run regularly or frequently. It was organized by a voluntary agency once in late 1993, a year after the implementation of the job search course. For their part, the skills upgrading courses are provided only by two training bodies, namely, the Hong Kong Productivity Council and the Hong Kong Seamen's Union. They are geared to the training needs of some technicians, but are not open for the general displaced workers.

Participation of Workers

Ironically, workers remain peripheral to the planning process of courses despite the central role they play in the ERS. Initially, there was no survey conducted on the needs and characteristics of the potential trainees by the government before the implementation of the scheme. The courses were planned mostly based on statistics of vacancies provided by official departments. Also, there were no plans to carry out any follow-up study to find out the marketability of the workers after retraining. Thus the workers have been almost incidental to the planning, implementation, and evaluation of the program.

Recently, the ERB recognized the necessity of addressing the displaced workers' needs and problems. It thus commissioned a university college to examine the needs of the trainees as well as employers' preferences for training. This report was scheduled to be out in 1995, some three years after the setting up of the scheme. The specifics of the report had not been discussed in public, reflecting the marginal status of such report. Moreover, it was soon overshadowed by another large-scale evaluation. In 1996, the government announced its wish to conduct a more thorough review of the program. Its recommendations came out in late 1996 (See Appendix 1 for full details of the recommendations). This latest report is silent on the issue of workers' participation. In the light of these developments, it can be surmised that this issue will be glossed over by the government.

In the past, it was very much dependent upon individual instructors to facilitate trainees in classroom participation. Often, as was experienced by a worker who completed an orientation course on job search lately, the trainees were not encouraged to speak up in class by the instructors who lectured most of the time. Some trainees find instructors more supportive of classroom participation but only in the form of questions about the specific skills. Furthermore, the trainees are usually not given any chance to express their opinions about the content or format of a course other than completing a course evaluation form at the end. Even this is limiting, as the evaluation form itself does not include many items or areas. Another trainee of a Chinese typewriting course found her instructor sympathetic to trainees' participation but only in the form of questions about their typewriting skills. There were no other forms of trainee participation.

Construction of Knowledge

Since the concept of knowledge construction is an abstract one, evidence can only be inferred from the formats of course delivery and the participation of workers in the program. As discussed above, the majority of the courses emphasize transmittance of skills from instructors to workers who are assigned a passive learning role in the classroom. Hence, the traits and experiences of the trainees are not considered as important factors in the construction of knowledge. Mr. T. S. Chow, Executive Director of the ERB, confirms this:

> Once workers are displaced, all their past working experience and skills are written off. And the ERB must also spend more time and resources to retrain them for a new job in a new field.[8]

It is therefore clear that the construction of knowledge is a single direction "instructor-to-trainees" style of teaching. As revealed by two trainees who provided the authors with information, their experiences were not regarded as relevant or respected during the training. It was pointed out that the instructor had no understanding about the background of the trainees as individuals. Neither did the instructor know any techniques to involve trainees in the generation of knowledge.

Concept of Management

The ERB adopts a top-down, employer-centered approach in the planning and implementation of the training scheme. The whole setup is not unlike other government bureaucracies. All 17 members of the ERB are appointed by the Hong Kong Governor and are supposed to be adequately representing perspectives of the government, employers, employees, and vocational training professionals. This group operates the scheme with information and support from other government departments and official statistics. There is no system to ensure consultation with the potential trainees or employers in the field. Not surprisingly, this hierarchical operation runs the risk of overlooking the needs of the individual workers and employers. During a Legislative Council meeting in May 1993, a member, Mr. Y. C. Tam, stated that:

> Achievements of the ERS are so far limited because there is no guidance from systematic market research and it has to feel its way to cross the river, so to speak.

Another Council member, Ronald Arculli, suggested that the low employment rate of the trainees could be due to many factors

> . . . including accurate estimate of the labour market demand, the practicability of the various courses offered, as well as the expectations of the retrainees.[9]

Obviously, the government had not given due consideration to those factors before launching the ERS.

This hierarchical structure of the ERS could mean that trainers increasingly would be removed from practical reality. This would result in trainees who have completed courses still not being able to meet other job requirements. For instance, courses on hotel housekeeping are popular in enrollment because there is a great demand for labor in the booming tourist industry. However, the trainees who were graduated from the courses have many difficulties in getting employment because many hotels only employ staff under 30 years old. Moreover, the work hours requiring shift work pose problems to many trainees who are middle-aged housewives. This lack of matching of the training courses to the life situations of the trainees and requirements of employers is one main reason accounting for the low employment rate of the retrained workers.[10] It also leads to criticisms against the ERB for pursuing retraining for the sake of retraining only, and acting like the proverbial man who built a carriage indoors and then found that it did not fit the road. The trainees become inadvertent victims of the mistakes made by the ERB's lack of foresight.

Conclusion

According to the above criteria, the ERS leans toward the traditional behavioral model of workplace training. This is, in large measure, attributed to the top-down bureaucratic nature of its program development. The emphasis in the ERS is on the adopting of new skills rather than enhancing learning capacity. From the perspective of Action Regulation Theory, the retraining program fails to acknowledge the facts that the learning process must refer to different levels of regulation and that there is an integration between acquisition of skills and acquisition of knowledge. Learners are not confronted with different action demands and the learning process is never aligned to a high level of self-reliance. For their part, proponents of critical reflectivity theory might challenge the scheme for its over-emphasis on instrumental learning while disregarding the levels of communicative learning and reflectivity. Separating one's learning from the learning context is intrinsically flawed. These two theories strongly suggest that the acquisition of knowledge, skills and personal development are all crucial to the training process. A narrow focus on skills training fails to prepare workers for the challenge of changing and varied work environments. Thus, in its conception, design, implementation and management, the ERS is short-sighted. Given its goals, this short-sightedness is the Achilles' heel of the whole project.

◆   ◆   ◆

NOTES

1. Hong Kong Legislative Council (1992). *Legislative Council Paper No. 945/91-92*. Hong Kong: Legco.

2. Hong Kong Legislative Council (1993). *Legislative Council Paper No. 3308/92-93*. Hong Kong: Legco.

3. Hong Kong Legislative Council (1993). *Legislative Council Paper No. 3821*. Hong Kong: Legco.

4. Hong Kong Legislative Council (1993). *Legislative Council Paper No. 3826*. Hong Kong: Legco.

5. Hong Kong Legislative Council (1993). *Legislative Council Proceedings*. May Sessions.

6. Employees Retraining Board (1993). *Course Description*. Hong Kong: Employees Retraining Board.

7. Construction Industry Training Association (1992). *Annual Report*. Hong Kong: CITA, p. 14.

8. *Hong Kong Productivity News*, October 1993, p. 4.

9. Hong Kong Legislative Council (1993). *Legislative Council Proceedings*. May Sessions.

10.   One adult educator in Hong Kong estimated that 30 percent of the workers who participated in the ERS since its inception have not found their jobs (*Oriental News*, December 25, 1996). A group of non-governmental organizations offering adult education would soon launch a large-scale needs study on lifelong education for Hong Kong citizens. If implemented, this will represent the very first attempt at charting lifelong education needs in Hong Kong.

CHAPTER FIVE

EMPLOYEES RETRAINING SCHEME: AN APPRAISAL

Program Effectiveness

The Employees Retraining Scheme has been criticized by advocates of free enterprise for investing in a socially inefficient project unless its involvement can result in efficiency gains over the private sector.[1] One major argument is that publicly funded training programs which do not require repayment by the trainees distort incentives and result in offsetting inefficiencies. Nonetheless, the government involvement in retraining is welcomed by other sectors in the job market. The big employers are relieved that the crisis of labor shortage has been met by provision of training and, more significantly, by the justification of importing cheap labor from China and other developing countries in Southeast Asia. At the same time, labor organizations in Hong Kong have been pressing the government to fund training for workers for years. Even though there are still flaws in the program, it is regarded as a breakthrough by the government. Hence, the issue to be reviewed here is the effectiveness of the ERS in meeting the needs of the unemployed workers, rather than to query whether such a scheme is necessary in the colony.

79

To illustrate some of the main drawbacks of the scheme from a worker's perspective, it is useful to examine the letter of a worker (aged 35, single female, with Grade 8 education). She had participated in a training course of the ERS and later wrote to a major newspaper about her experiences. She was very frustrated and felt insulted because:

> . . . the instructor of the course asked us to do some self-understanding exercises to find out whether we are "artistic, extrovert or introvert" to decide whether we are suitable for professions such as that of doctor, fashion designer, social worker and accountant. How sarcastic! . . . I have over twenty years of social experiences. Would the employers recognize that? . . . The Labour Department has organized job referral exhibitions in some high-class places . . . Every time we were told to fill out forms and return home to wait, but a reply never came . . . I arranged by myself interviews as salesperson, cashier, waitress etc. But I wasn't hired because I am too "old" and not well educated . . . . But what is depressing is the fact that the instructor remarked that it is very difficult to obtain jobs through the assistance of ERB and Labour Department because those factories which seek workers through registration with the government actually look for cheap imported labour as their priority.
>
> *Ming Pao Daily News*[2]

There are several important points raised by the above worker. First, the course contents were not relevant to the life situation of the workers. Second, the strengths and experiences of the worker were not recognized. Third, the job referral system of the government was not meeting needs or the culture of workers. Fourth, the course, by focusing on interview skills, was overlooking both the characteristics of the trainees as well as the reality of the job market. All these points reflect the problems of program planning in an hierarchical and skills-oriented model. This mismatch of skills training and market demand is echoed in the findings of a survey study of manufacturing workers by one labor group in Hong Kong. The Lai

Chi Kok Labour Group interviewed 264 people on their attitudes toward retraining.[3] Some 78 percent of the respondents indicated they would need retraining if they changed jobs. About half had considered taking up new jobs. Only 6.7 percent of the respondents had undergone retraining previously. Yet some 23 percent expressed a lack of confidence in ERS to enable them to look for new jobs. Lastly, most participants thought that trainees should be employed by those employers who choose to import labor, thus showing their resentment against the government's labor importation policy.

Despite all these problems, government leadership in the retraining of workers in Hong Kong is timely. At present, there is insufficient training provision for workers in the formal education system (universities, polytechnic, quasi-governmental organizations, etc.). As well, the scale of training requirements (displaced workers, regular skill upgrading, etc.) is very large. As it stands, only very large firms can afford to spend money on retraining of their workers. Thus, the training opportunities provided by the private sector are limited and diminishing because of the large number of small firms in the Colony and the relocation of plants to other countries where cheap labor is in abundant supply.

In addition, government intervention in workers' training is advantageous, in that it provides a broad overview of where the economy is heading. The Hong Kong government has been criticized for its policy of non-intervention compared to the policies of neighboring nations like Japan and Singapore which have been investing larger amounts in the nurturing of a highly skilled workforce. As the government is playing a more active role in economic development, it is natural that it should provide leadership in workers' retraining to match changing labour needs.

From the perspectives of the labor sector, the ERS is socially desirable. Most trainees have worked for a long time to contribute to the prosperity of the colony. Yet the welfare policy of Hong Kong provides them with little security. They are simply replaced when cheap labor is available outside the territory. Therefore, the ERS is welcomed as a long-term financial commitment of the government to the welfare of the workers.

Hence, the retraining scheme is not without its merits. Furthermore, in response to criticisms, there have been some changes made as the scheme has evolved. It has expanded to cover housewives and the disabled, the number of courses have been increased to provide more variety, and surveys and studies are being conducted to obtain more information on the trainees. One particularly good move is the setting up of an On-the-Job Training Program (OJT) in which employers are subsidized to employ and train displaced workers. Even though the program is still not well developed (i.e., only those "employable" workers can find jobs and some employers terminate the employment as soon as the training period ends and the subsidy stops), it is a step away from the very skill-oriented "Training first, job seeking afterwards" approach. More importantly, it indicates that the government recognizes the need for learning in the workplace and is looking for different training models. Furthermore, a few training bodies have begun to incorporate some social elements in their skills training courses to enhance the self-understanding and interview skills of trainees.

However, piecemeal changes in the ERS or improvements made by some individual training agencies will not be sufficient. There are demands for more active government involvement in the labor market. A survey conducted by the Clothing Industry Workers' General Union and the Confederation of Trade Unions in December, 1993[4] has found that most employers prefer to hire workers in their late teens or early twenties, and more than 70 percent of employers in the retail sector and 60 percent seeking junior clerks and telephone operators have set an upper age limit of 30. This age discrimination poses great difficulty for many ERS trainees in getting new jobs. In other words, government intervention through legislation and a comprehensive review of the programming of the ERS are necessary in order to ensure employment opportunities for the retrained workers.

Need for Change

Like other social services in Hong Kong, the ERS follows a remedial approach to solve social problems. The need for retraining, particularly in the clothing manufacturing industry, has been voiced for a long time. However, the government insisted on non-intervention until the problem dramatically escalated due to the importation of foreign workers and the subsequent angry voices became too loud to be ignored. As discussed, the ERS was launched in haste and without involving workers and employers. Hence, the scheme has been criticized by some people as a move of tokenism rather than a genuine attempt to take care of the interests of workers. Nevertheless, the authors suggest that a retraining policy is required to provide direction and a framework of public-funded programs. Therefore, what follows is a list of the essential elements in a well formulated worker training policy:

1.   It provides an overall view about anticipated future changes in economy and labor demands.

2.   It is proactive in approach. It should match with economic development and provide retraining opportunities to adapt to movements in the job market.

3.   It should be ongoing and not stop after workers find new employment.

4.   Labor training or retraining should not be made available to displaced workers only. It should cover the general labor population.

5.   Training programs initiated by private employers should be encouraged and supported.

6.   The right and opportunities for workers to attend training programs should be protected by legislation.

On the programming level, the Hong Kong government tends to follow a conventional and conservative approach which is similar to the behavioral model of labor training. The over-emphasis on skills training has been proven to be insufficient to prepare workers to gain new employment. There have been recommendations that the programs should be worker-centered and the planning should start at the bottom instead of from the top. Hence, the emerging paradigms of training such as those discussed in Chapter Two should be studied with the Hong Kong situation in mind to improve existing practice. A more worker-centered approach is required particularly in the following phases of program planning:

Needs Assessment

Worker participation should be involved at different stages including planning, on-going review and evaluation. As a group, workers are in the best position to tell what the barriers to attending the training program are. Also, with information from the government and their workplaces, workers are able to contribute to the establishment of training programs that meet their own needs. Therefore, survey studies on the expressed needs of potential trainees, consumer studies, records of the employment status of workers completing the programs, and involvement of trainees in mid-course feedback are some of the means to increase participation of workers.

Course Objective

One objective should be to enhance trainees' general competency at the workplace. It is particularly important to workers in Hong Kong to learn how to learn since the job market is constantly evolving, adapting to the political and economic climate in China. The rapid advances in technology and the provision of intensive labor outside the territory lead to new modes of production. Therefore, the workers need to acquire a capacity to take up new roles and to apply their generic skills and work experiences to new work situations. In other words, the retraining program should not only aim at relocation of workers but also at enhancing their competitiveness in the market. Otherwise, these workers will keep coming back to the program as labor demands in Hong Kong shift all the time.

Course Content

The strengths and work experiences of the workers must be given due respect and recognition in course design. The course content should be extended from a skills emphasis to cover cultivation of appropriate work attitudes. Organizations nowadays emphasize a more collaborative approach, using people-skills, critical thinking and commitment at the workplace. These requirements are different from the past when workers were only requested to perform assigned tasks. It is most important, therefore, for those displaced workers to tune into the culture of their selected new trades. Without understanding the relationship between skills and the activities in which they are used in a social job context, the workers will not be able to perform the jobs properly, even though they may have the required technical skills.

Instruction Method and Course Delivery

Individual preferences of learners should be taken into consideration at this phase. To be learner-centered means to accept the fact that people learn best in different ways. Traditional classroom teaching may not be the most appropriate setting for workers' training in all cases. The provision of courses in various formats and settings, particularly in contexts close to real workplaces, would facilitate more effective learning. More courses, for example, could follow the lead of the On-the-Job Training (OJT) Program as to situated learning.[5] Further, an increase in variety to meet different learning needs and styles is necessary, regardless of course content.

Training of Instructors

The instructors should be able to identify different learning needs and styles of their trainees in order to be effective. Some trainees may have emotional and social blockages to learning new trades due to their life experiences and status as displaced workers. The ERB so far has depended on individual training bodies to run their own courses, recruit trainees and keep track of graduates. Yet there is no support or resources given to the training of trainers to orientate them to the characteristics of their potential trainees. This likely poses a serious constraint to the effectiveness of the whole scheme in the long run.

Conclusion

Over the past several years, competitive job market conditions and the absence of government intervention have limited Hong Kong's working class in keeping pace with the prosperous but changing economy. As a consequence, a large group of workers have been "displaced" and discarded from the employment market. The establishment of the ERS is a remedial step taken by the government in a critical political situation. Labor sector views the fundamental problem of worker displacement as caused by the labor importation scheme. The "imported" workers, who fill up the semi-skilled or unskilled jobs, erode the existing labor structure and take away job opportunities of local workers. It also leads to another social issue, namely, the exploitation of the imported workers who are paid at wage levels not acceptable to local workers. Hence, the labor training in Hong Kong is closely tied to the overall labor and economic policy and any changes in one area will affect development in others. This calls for the formulation of an active labor market policy[6], which takes into account economic and political factors, to protect the interests of the workers. By itself, the ERS can only be a short-term solution if it is not backed up by a long-term policy.

To a certain extent, the ERS represents a new era of labor development in Hong Kong, since it is the first large-scale government intervention in workers' training. The effectiveness of the scheme, however, is limited by the behavioral approach at every level of the scheme from its overall planning to the level of course delivery. Under strong criticism, the scheme has been expanded to cover a larger clientele and provide more courses in various settings. However, fundamental changes in the training model have to be made in order to meet the requirements of modern work qualifications. Specialized skills training is no longer sufficient to ensure work competency. Other key work qualifications include the broadening of skills for an individual to adjust into different job cultures. The behavioral model is found to be weak and ineffective for inculcating these more attitudinal aspects of work. Indeed, there may not be one model that can address the complex employment problems in Hong Kong. Yet the selective incorporation of various models to meet the evolving needs of workplace training would prove to be more conducive to learning than reliance on a single approach. Therefore, further studies in this area are highly recommended.

To conclude, it is important for Hong Kong to develop a policy and framework of worker training in view of its trends of social, economic and political development. All of these trends are intertwined and affect one another. The demographic change in Hong Kong has transformed the workforce profile into one composed of younger people with higher education. As a group, they are more vocal and assertive, particularly in striving for better welfare, training and job prospects. On the other hand, China is developing into a huge manufacturing base with its intensive labor and low production costs. This pushes Hong Kong to move towards being a center of technological and management services supporting the mainland. Training and retraining of workers, therefore, will be essential to maintain a high-level workforce able to keep pace with evolving technological advances. The government and big firms will be expected and obligated to invest more in human resources development.

Politically, Hong Kong will be returned to the sovereignty of China in 1997. The Chinese government has policies different from Hong Kong regarding labor relations, workers' insurance and workplace training. Even though there is a Sino-British agreement to ensure that Hong Kong will maintain its own economic system for the next fifty years, it seems inevitable that in the future the government of Hong Kong will follow the lead of China in taking up a central role in the area of workplace training. However, uncertainty lingers due to great upheavals and changes in the political arena of China as well as the deteriorating relationship between the Chinese and the present Hong Kong government in the past years.[7] Therefore, despite the fact that a lot still depends on the smooth transition of the colony back to the sovereignty of its mother country in 1997, an established policy and framework of workforce training may help in providing Hong Kong some consistency in a period of uncertainty.

◆   ◆   ◆

NOTES

1. William Chan (1993). "Retraining the Unemployed in Hong Kong." *HKCER Letters*. Hong Kong Center for Economic Research.

2. *Ming Pao Daily News*, October 28, 1993.

3. Lai Chi Kok Labor Group (1993). *Survey on Employees Retraining in Hong Kong*. August.

4. Construction Industry Training Authority (1993). *Annual Report*. Hong Kong: CITA.

5. This suggestion runs counter to the recent recommendations of the consultancy report 1996 which calls for phasing out such programs. The reason for such phasing out is both financial and administrative: ". . . (As) the ERB has little control over the quality and effectiveness of the training provided to the trainee once he or she has been employed on-the-job, the OJT has turned out to be largely a system of financial subsidy for employers . . ." (Recommendation 8).

6. Active Labour Market Policy (ALMP) is defined by Thomas Janoski (1994) as "direct government intervention into labor markets to decrease unemployment through job-placement, job-training, and job-creation programs." Scandinavian countries have ALMP in place while countries like the United States, Iceland, Greece and Australia have not devoted much financial resources to such programs. The idea of ALMP has not been seriously discussed in Hong Kong nor other East Asian NICs.

7. Since the arrival of Christopher Patten, the last governor of Hong Kong, Britain and China have had incessant debates over many political issues. The bone of contention has been the colonial government's attempts at democratisation of the political structure. For instance, more members of the Legislative Council are now elected through direct election. China is very suspicious of such moves, believing that they are conspiracies on the part of the British government to "stir up" troubles before its departure on June 30, 1997.

CHAPTER SIX

POSTSCRIPT

I should like to reiterate that measures such as the Employees Retraining
Scheme have proved to be genuinely useful in helping displaced workers
to re-enter the job market.
> T. H. Chau, Acting Financial Secretary, "Economic Strategy"
> Speech to the Legislative Council on June 14, 1995.

Training and Retraining are a vital part of Hong Kong's future economic
prospects. I think that increasingly a community's prosperity is going to
be determined by the skill level and knowledge level in the country and
we've got to move fast to make sure that we always improve and
modernise our own training and retraining.
> Governor Christopher Patten, Public Meeting, October 2, 1996.

Recent Changes

Ever since the 1960s, the government has been committed to
investments in human capital. It sees formal education and training as
essential support to the economic growth. But it has not wanted to actively
involve itself in the labor market and has pursued instead a long-standing
policy of non-interventionism. This stand has been well supported by
business and industrialists. In spite of this, with some reluctance, the ERS
was set up in late 1992 to assist displaced workers to acquire new skills that
are valued in the marketplace. Since its establishment, the government has
praised the suitability of this policy. Now, the government comments that

retraining and job matching are the keys to helping the labour market work more efficiently and more humanely. They are among the highest priorities of the Government today.

Most recently, there have been other developments which underline the importance of retraining workers. First of all, the unexpected surge in the unemployment rate in 1995 caused lots of public concern. The unemployment rate reached 3.6 percent (September 1995) and stayed above 3.0 percent for 14 months before falling back to 2.9 percent. This translates to a change in the number of unemployed people from 110,000 to around 90,000 at the last count in September 1996. Compared to standards in industrialized countries, this rate is more than acceptable. However, Hong Kong has previously had a relatively long period of low unemployment at 2.0 percent; thus, this situation is unacceptable to the workers and their unions.

As a result of rising unemployment, the government implemented a series of measures. First, it tackled the problem of illegal employment which had undermined the interests of local workers. It increased fines on employers who had taken advantage of the shortage of labor by hiring illegal workers from China who were willing to work for very low pay. The second measure was to freeze the General Labour Importation Scheme in the summer of 1995, and to replace it by a smaller and more targeted Supplementary Labour Scheme in January, 1996.

More importantly, the government pledged its strong support for the ERS and saw it as the main solution to unemployment. It thus introduced a program which helped displaced workers find jobs by expanding the job matching and placement services. In April, 1995, the ERS launched a Job

Matching Programme jointly with the Labour Department with a view to providing active placement assistance to unemployed local job-seekers aged 30 or above through direct job referral or referral to tailor-made retraining courses. The government introduced this service at all nine Local Employment Service offices in August, 1995 and extended the program to all job-seekers irrespective of age in February, 1996.[1]

However, the ERB has been plagued by other problems. Above all, it has faced a chronic financial problem, due to two reasons. First, given the range of courses which generate few financial resources from the participants, the initial capital fund was quickly exhausted and the Board had to appeal to the government for further financial support. Second, when the government curtailed the General Labour Importation Scheme, the sharp drop in imported workers meant a drop in levies obtained from the employers. As a result of these two factors, an extra HK$300 million (US$38 million) was injected into the Employees Retraining Scheme by the government in 1996.

Despite these difficulties, a glance at the recent programming reveals the ERS has continued to expand coverage. In fact, the government has argued that

> it is imperative that we give people more retraining — the blind, the mentally-handicapped, the mentally-ill —so that they can contribute as much as they have got to the rest of society.

At the time of publication, it is also considering giving training to recent immigrants from China. While extending the coverage to more people is commendable, it is also clear that the ERS is heavily preoccupied with the maintaining high numbers of participants.

Consultancy Study

In 1996, the government declared its intention to conduct a review of the ERS and hired a consultancy firm for this purpose. The review is designed to improve the effectiveness of ERS in equipping workers to re-enter the workforce and to review the existing program in order to chart the way ahead. Regarding the consultancy study, the Secretary for Education and Manpower, Joseph Wong, opined that the government wants

> to ensure the provision of the most efficient, cost-effective and market responsible training and retraining programmes for our workers well into the 21st century.[2]

The government intends to use this review to form the basis for a longer-term employment and vocational training strategy. Governor Patten has promised to consult the public on the findings of the consultancy study when it comes out.

It should be noted that the ERS is not the only area in labor services which the government wants to evaluate. In fact, it has asked the consultancy firm to look at two other issues: vocational education and age discrimination in employment. The study of age discrimination in employment came out in the summer of 1996[3] and engendered an interesting reaction. Although the report does acknowledge the presence of age discrimination in some sectors, the government decided against legislative redress because public consultation which followed the release of the report was mixed. In the end, the government has favored public education and trusted that free play of the market would itself take care of the problem. This report is thus a big disappointment to critics since it simply means the continuation of social non-interventionism from the government. It is highly possible that the consultancy report on the ERS will have a similarly slight impact if the government takes the same attitude and avoids further active involvement in workers' retraining.

Such inertia on the part of the government is not surprising given that time is running out for the colonial administration. China will take over Hong Kong in mid-1997. Among top colonial administrators, there is therefore a strong impetus to maintain the status quo in order to avoid possible disruptions during the political transition.

Recommendations from the Consultancy Report — 1996

In early December 1996, after a long wait, the government finally released the consultancy report written by an accountancy firm Deloitte Toche Tohmatsu. The major recommendations include the following:[4]

1. The government is to pump an extra HK$500 million (US$64 million) into the ERS.
2. Immigrants from China will be allowed to take part in retraining.
3. The ERS will be revamped and it will focus on providing retraining for the "hard core unemployed," i.e., those who are over 30 and who have only lower secondary education.
4. Phasing out the existing ERB on-the-job program.

5.   Transferring the ERB's role in skills upgrading for the unemployed
        to the Vocational Training Council in phases.

6.   Reducing the existing retraining allowance from HK$4,000 (US$517)
        to HK$2,000 (US$258) a month.

7.   Introducing a placement-tied and performance-based payment system
        for training bodies to encourage them to find jobs for trainees.

8.   Improving the monitoring of training bodies.

Essentially, the government has indicated that it would provide
HK$500 million (US$64 million) in extra funding for the ERB. Further, it
will amend the existing Employees Retraining Ordinance to allow Chinese
immigrants to join the retraining scheme. Thus, these two recommendations
will be acted upon quickly by the government. As for the other
recommendations, their status remains to be decided. Probably, the Hong
Kong government needs more time to weigh the pros and cons of each
recommendation. Initial responses to the consultancy report from ERB and
labor groups are numerous and in the main negative.[5] Of significance is the
comment from the present chairman of the ERB, Mr. Tam Yiu-chung. He
welcomed the government's new cash infusion but he was very concerned
the fund would be wiped out within the next few years. Such depletion is
more likely now that the scheme has expanded to cover Chinese immigrants.
Generally, labor groups share this criticism and demand clarification from
government on this issue.

A long-time critic of the government, the Confederation of Trade
Unions has a number of strong criticisms of the report.[6] First of all, it
shares the worries of the ERB's chairman that the government's added

funding would be used up quickly. Since the government does not spell out how this cash infusion is arranged and whether it will be an ongoing one, there is the suspicion that the government wants to roll back its commitment to the ERS by cutting back its subsidies. It also feels that workers would be discouraged to join the scheme because of the smaller allowance. Given the high costs of living, it is doubtful if such a small allowance will help those people undergo retraining. The government is also seen as downsizing the ERS by transferring skills upgrading training from the ERS to the Vocational Training Council. More importantly, the Vocational Training Council is likely to resort to user fees for this kind of training. Given that, a lot of those poor unemployed workers will be excluded. Many are not eligible to take courses from the Vocational Training Council since it has maintained a high eligibility standard for its trainees, i.e., senior high school levels. Unquestionably, the integrity of the new ERS will be undermined by all these changes. Overall, the Confederation of Trade Unions charges that the Hong Kong government does not have any long-term policy for retraining and it is only for those unemployed workers. The government lacks a clear vision for training of workers in Hong Kong.

If the consultants want to have a comprehensive review, it would make good sense to solicit the views of the participants of the ERS. Unfortunately, there is no mention in the consultancy report that their review has involved the current and past trainees. It can be surmised that they are not consulted. Likewise, another critical actor — training agencies — are neglected by the consultant. Given their involvement and experiences, there is no reason that they should not be involved in the review process.[7] Furthermore, the consultant company sees job placement as an important tool in assessing the effectiveness of the training agencies. However, the introduction of a placement-tied payment system would run the risks of making training agencies serve only those who are able to find work quickly. Those who are not able to do so will be very vulnerable and excluded from retraining. A strong but undue emphasis is thus placed on successful placement rate of the retrainees.

Prevailing Criticisms

One will have to wait to hear more public feedback to the consultancy report. Since the inception of the ERS, there have been no lack of critics of the program. Some critics have charged the ERB for insufficient training capacity in view of the long queue for the most popular courses; in some cases, applicants have had to wait for up to a year to get a place. As noted above, funding has been somewhat haphazard and the training itself, when it is done, has not reflected a worker-centered or carefully crafted economic or vocational strategy. Also, there is evidence that significant numbers of trainees have not been able to find jobs in the field in which they were trained. One critic summarizes the flaws and also notes some abuses of the program:

> The government-sponsored retraining schemes [have been] criticized as ineffectual, since the content of those programmes were considered too irrelevant or too basic to help secure a job after the training period. What was most likely to happen, however, was the use of trainees to fill short-term vacancies; since the Employees Retraining Board subsidized one-third of the employees' wages for the first three months, unscrupulous employers would not hesitate to take advantage of the scheme.[8]

But how would the ERB assess itself? A 1994 internal evaluation report provides some clues. The ERB professes a strong commitment to the market-driven approach which permeates its operational strategy and course design. This approach is justified, claims the report, since the market is assumed to be the most reliable pointer as to whether the program is going in the right direction. Thus the ERB apparently believes that the employer is best positioned to (1) know its own training needs, (2) know the training needs of the workers, and (3) provide the appropriate training.

Thus, there is no question that the ERS is essentially top-down and market-driven in its implementation strategy. However, there are some instances when the ERB, which does not adopt a worker-centered approach, comes to realize that active learning on the part of workers is essential. For instance, workers who attended the Job Search Skills courses found it difficult to adapt to one-day classroom sessions and preferred more group discussions and social activities. As a consequence, this course was restructured by condensing the classroom sessions to a half day while leaving the other half day in field work. The retrainees were organized into small support groups for field work and discussions.

Unfortunately, this kind of example of adjusting the ERS courses is rare. With the conspicuous absence of worker-centered philosophy in the ERS, it is hard to see more examples of this kind. It is true that one labor leader, Mr. Tam Yiu-chung, is appointed by the government and he now serves as the Chairman of the ERB. Some critical assessments of the ERS have been coming from him. For instance, he has commented correctly on the lack of long-term planning for this program. However, the ERB is still over-committed to documenting the number of retrainees and following those who have found jobs, rather than looking at ways to improve the program. The crucial aspect of the program — the nature of training — is glossed over. This neglect only reflects the fact that the ERS is market-driven in its direction, with an implicit acceptance of the behavioral model of training. A critical assessment of the nature of retraining is long overdue.

NOTES

1.   Hong Kong Government (1996). *Hong Kong Annual Report 1996*. Hong Kong: Government Printer.

2.   Secretary for Education and Manpower Joseph Wong Wing-Ping's Speech, September 1996.

3.   Hong Kong Government (1994). *Equal Opportunities: A Study on Discrimination in Employment on the Ground of Age*. Hong Kong: Government Printer.

4.   Hong Kong Government (1996). *Review of the Employees Retraining Scheme: A Consultation Paper*. Hong Kong: Education and Manpower Branch. See Appendix for fuller details of these recommendations.

5.   *Labor Movement Monthly*. January/February Issues, 1997.

6.   *Labor Movement Monthly*. January/February Issues, 1997.

7.   Hong Kong Council of Social Service. Special Issue on Unemployment. *Welfare Digest*, February, 1997, p. 3.

8.   Tong, Irene (1994). "Women" in Donald McMillen and Si-wai Man (Eds.) *The Other Hong Kong Report 1994*, pp. 367-88. Hong Kong: Chinese University of Hong Kong Press.

APPENDIX 1

Selected Recommendations from the
Consultancy Report 1996
(Review of the Employees Retraining Scheme)

Target Retrainees

2.   We propose that the retraining programme provided under the Employees Retraining Scheme should primarily focus on those unemployed who are aged 30 and above, have received lower secondary education or below (i.e. Secondary 3 education or below), have the legal right to seek employment with any employers in Hong Kong (i.e. including new immigrants) and who are actively looking for employment. However, we recommend that the age and educational attainment criteria could be applied flexibly by the ERB in individual cases, particularly for new immigrants, given their different educational and vocational backgrounds. With these proposed changes, the ERS will, in effect, assume the distinctive role of providing retraining for the unemployed in the overall system of vocational training and retraining in Hong Kong.

3.   According to the latest unemployment statistics, the number of unemployed persons who have educational attainment at Secondary 3 or below (some of whom could be new immigrants) was 49,400 in the second quarter of 1996. Of these, 32,300 were aged 30-59 and this category of unemployed consistently accounts for about 35% of all unemployed persons in Hong Kong.

4.   As for new immigrants, they comprise mainly legal immigrants from China. During the seven years up to September, 1996, a total of 256,460 legal immigrants from China entered Hong Kong through the PRC one-way permit system. Of the 73,495 such immigrants admitted between 1 July 1995 and 30 September 1996, 28,628 (or 39%) are aged 25 to 64 and have no more than secondary education. However, there are no statistics on how many new immigrants are unemployed. Based on the current quota of 150 a day, about 55,000 legal immigrants from China will be admitted into Hong Kong each year.

5.   We propose that the ERS should focus on the unemployed, including new immigrants. The target group should primarily be those who are aged 30 or above and have attained lower secondary education or below. There are four reasons:

a)   This group forms the bulk of the unemployed.

b)   Since this group is at the lower end of the social and educational spectrum, they constitute the 'hard-core' of the unemployed who are most vulnerable to the adverse effects of any structural change in the economy and who also stand the highest chance of being displaced from the labour market.

c)   On account of their educational and occupational background, many new immigrants may not possess the requisite skills required to find employment in the local labour market. They should therefore also be eligible to benefit from the ERS.

d)   At present, no publicly-funded vocational training institutions provide job-oriented training programme specifically for those (including the employed and the unemployed) with less than Secondary 3 education. The minimum entry requirements of the training programmes currently provided by the Vocational Training Council are set at the completion of Secondary 3 or equivalent level.

6.   In order to focus the ERS on training the 'hard core' of the unemployed and the new immigrants, we propose that all the skills upgrading courses for the employed persons, and the ancillary retraining courses for the elderly and the disabled now being offered under the ERS, should in future be provided by the Vocational Training Council instead. Given its remit, experience and facilities, the Vocational Training Council should be well placed and equipped to fulfil this role. With this clear demarcation of training responsibilities and target clienteles, the ERB and the Vocational Training Council will be able to develop and build on their individual strengths. Besides, any possible duplication of efforts between the ERB and the Vocational Training Council could be avoided. This will also enable the ERB to re-deploy some 40% of its current annual expenditure (around $110 million in 1995-96) on skills upgrading to the development of better-quality retraining programme for the unemployed and for training, more people, including new immigrants.

Course structure and Contents

7.   We propose that the training programme should take the form of a specially-designed and structured package of job-oriented intensive training courses with the objective of facilitating the target group of unemployed to

secure employment and hold down their jobs. [We] consider that the programme should consist of three components:

i)   General induction training for, say, one week.

ii)   Job-specific skills training for, say, three to four weeks on average, with the actual duration depending on the type and nature of skills training.

(The type of job-specific skills could be selected on the basis of the job vacancies available in the local labour market, and on the results of the Survey on Employment and Vacancies undertaken by the Census and Statistics Department, and the Local Employment Service of the Labour Department. The views of employers including those represented on the ERB should be taken fully into account.)

iii) Initial follow-up training and counselling shortly after a retrainee has been placed in a job.

Special remedial sessions could also be provided to cater for the specific needs of individual applicants and new immigrants, as and when necessary. Retrainees who have completed this retraining programme should be placed in jobs through the relevant training bodies as far as practicable. To prevent abuse and to optimise the use of retraining resources, we propose that any person who has completed retraining (including the proposed initial follow-up training) will not be allowed to have access to the ERS within a period of two years.

8.   Currently, the ERB runs an On-the-Job programme (OJT) which aims at encouraging employers to hire and train ERB trainees. Financial subsidy up to a maximum of $4,000 per month for a duration of six months is paid to the employer as an incentive and to offset part of the cost of employing the trainees. However, as the ERB has little control over the quality and effectiveness of the training provided to the trainee once he or she has been employed on-the-job, the OJT has turned out to be largely a system of financial subsidy for employers. We propose to phase out the existing OJT programme and replace it with the specially designed training programme for the unemployed as set out in paragraph 7 above.

Retraining Allowance

9.   The retraining allowance under the existing ERS is designed to serve as an incentive to induce the unemployed to receive retraining with a view to seeking work by providing them with a financial subsidy for the duration of their training. At present, this is set at about $1,000 per week for those attending full-time training courses. For courses less than 40 hours, the retrainees only receive the allowance if they can find a job upon completion of training.

10.   To strike a balance between the need to provide an allowance to enable the proposed target group of hard-core unemployed (who are at the lower end of our social and educational spectrum) to receive retraining, and the need to prevent possible abuse, we propose to replace the existing retraining allowance by a new allowance of $500 per week payable to all retrainees to cover the travelling and meal expenses incurred by them whilst

attending retraining. This would result in some savings in the payment of allowance which could then be re-deployed to fund the enhanced and expanded retraining programme.

Role of ERB

11.   At present, the ERB provides funding support to training bodies which provide retraining courses at their training centres. We propose that the ERB should continue to be a contracting and funding agency instead of a direct provider of training.

12.   [We] propose that the ERB should critically evaluate the number and composition of the training bodies with a view to improving their effectiveness and monitoring the performance of such training bodies and the quality of the training provided. At present, training bodies are nearly all non-governmental organisations. Six major institutions provide 79% of the training, while 49 others provide the remaining 21%.

A placement-tied and performance-based payment system for training bodies

13.   At present, training bodies are reimbursed by the ERB fully for the cost they incur in providing courses and on the basis of enrolment. The quality and quantity of employment output generated has little to do with payments. We propose to replace this arrangement by a performance-based payment system for training bodies to ensure that the type of training provided to the target retrainees is placement-focused and job-oriented. Specifically, the payment to training bodies for training provided should be made on the basis of the number of trainees who have completed training

and successfully secured job placement. All training bodies will be required to attain a reasonable percentage of placements for their trainees. Those training bodies which are capable of over-achieving the target placement rate will receive a higher than normal reimbursement by the ERB as a financial incentive while those which have under-achieved the target will receive less and will have their performance critically reviewed by the ERB to see whether they should continue to participate in the ERS.

14.   Under the proposal, the ERB will survey costs and average placement rates for retraining courses. For example, a particular course might cost $210,000 to train 20 people and on average 14 placements (70% of the course participants) could be achieved. Under the current practice, the sum of $210,000 is paid to the training body as long as enrolment reaches the 20-person target. Under the proposed system, payments would only be made for each person who completes training and is successfully placed in jobs. Payments per placement would be calculated by dividing the total cost ($210,000) by the 14 trainees expected to be placed in an average performing course. The ERB would then pay $15,000 ($210,000/14) for every person who completes training and is placed. If the training body places more than 14 trainees, it receives more money than it would under the current system. If it places fewer trainees, the training body receives less. The ERB can make cash flow payments during the course of training, but the money cannot be counted as earned income until the performance requirements are met. In this context, a successful placement for funding purposes is defined as one where the employment of the retrainee and retention on the job following placement should last for at least two to three

months. Where possible, the retrainee should be placed in a job related to the skills training he has received.

15.   The placement results of the training bodies will facilitate the ERB to assess the effectiveness of the training courses in achieving their intended objective. This system is not merely an accounting change. Rather, it is a shifting of risk and reward to the training bodies. As a result, training bodies will be given more freedom to design courses and assign trainees to various courses. The ERB's role will also shift to a greater monitoring and oversight of employment outcomes, rather than course selection and review of training inputs.

◆   ◆   ◆

BIBLIOGRAPHY

Adams, Roy (Ed.) (1991). *Comparative Industrial Relations: Contemporary Research and Theory.* London: Harper Collins.

Addison, John T. & Siebert, Stanley (1994). "Vocational Training and the European Community." *Oxford Economic Papers*, 46(4), October, pp. 696-724.

Alfthan, T. & Jonzon, B. (1994). "Retraining Adult Workers in Sweden," *Training Policy Study* No. 3. Geneva: International Labor Office.

American Society for Training and Development (1986). *Serving The New Corporation.* Alexandria, VA: American Society for Training and Development.

American Society for Training and Development (1994). "The Coming of Age of Workplace Learning: A Time Line." *Training and Development*, 48, pp. 4-21.

American Society for Training and Development (1996). *Assessing Training Needs.* Alexandria, VA: Author.

Amjad, R. & Mohanty, M. (1991). *Industrial Restructuring and Implications for Human Resource Development in ASEAN.* New Delhi: Asian HRD Networking Paper, ILO-ARTEP.

Anderson, Garry E. (1993). *Shouldn't You Own Your Future Today? Linking Education to Skills in Quality Organization.* Milwaukee: ASQC/ Quality Press.

Ashley-Oahm, Dayna (1994). *Adult Workers: Retraining the American Workforce.* Denver: National Conference of State Legislature.

109

Auer, P. (1993). "Continuing Training for the Employed in Europe." *inforMISEP*, No. 42. Brussels, Commission of the European Communities.

Axel, H. (1989). *Job Banks for Retirees*. New York: The Conference Board.

Bailey, Paul et al. (1993). *Multinationals and Employment — The Global Economy of the 1990s*. Geneva: International Labor Office.

Baldwin, J. R. & Gorecki, P. K. (1990). *Structural Change and the Adjustment Process: Perspectives on Firm Growth and Worker Turnover*. Ottawa: Statistics Canada and Economic Council of Canada.

Bartam, Sharon (1994). *Training Needs Analysis: A Resource for Identifying Training Needs. Selecting Strategies and Developing Training Needs*. Brookfield: Ashgate.

Bartel, A. P. (1989). *Formal Employee Training Program and Their Impact on Labor Productivity: Evidence from a Human Resources Survey*. Cambridge: National Bureau of Economic Research.

Barton, Paul E. (1986). *A Better Fit Between Unemployment Insurance and Retraining*. Washington, D.C.: National Institute For Work and Learning.

Bassi, L. J. (1994). "Workplace Education for Hourly Workers." *Journal of Policy Analysis and Management*, 13(1), pp. 55-74.

Becker, G. S. (1975). *Human Capital: A Theoretical and Empirical Analysis with Special Reference to Education*. New York: National Bureau of Economic Research.

Bermant, Mikhail & Feonova, Marina (1991). *Training and Retraining: The Link with Employment*. USSR Academy of Sciences: State Committee for Labor & Social Affairs.

Bhola, H. S. (1988). *World Trends and Issues in Adult Education.* United Nations: UNESCO.

Birren, J. E., Robinson, P. K. & Livingstone, J. E. (Eds.) (1986). *Age, Health, and Employment.* Englewood Cliffs: Prentice-Hall.

Bloom, Howard S. (1984). "Estimating the Effect of Job-Training Programs, Using Longitudinal Data: Ashenfelter's Findings Reconsidered." *Journal of Human Resources,* 19(4), pp. 544-546.

Bloom, Howard S. (1990). *Back to Work: Testing Reemployment Services for Displaced Workers.* Kalamazoo, Michigan: W. E. Upjohn Institute for Employment Research.

Borus, Michael E. (1979). *Measuring the Impact of Employment Related Social Programs: A Primer.* Kalamazoo, Michigan: W. F. Upjohn Institute for Employment.

Borus, Michael E. (1983). *Tomorrow's Workers.* Lexington: Lexington Books.

Bosch, Gerhard (1990). *Retraining - Not Redundancy: Innovative Approaches to Industrial Restructuring in Germany and France.* Geneva: International Institute for Labor Studies, International Labor Office.

Burtless, G. (1983). *Why Is Insured Unemployment So Low?* Brookings Papers on Economic Activity, No. 1, pp. 225-249. Washington, D.C.: The Brookings Institution.

Business Council for Effective Literacy (1993). *The Connection Between Employee Basic Skills and Productivity.* New York: BCEL Brief.

Candor, Leonard (1989). *Vocational Education and Training in the Developed World: A comparative Study.* New York: Routledge.

Candy, Philip (1991). *Self-Direction for Life-long Learning: A Comprehensive Guide to Theory and Practice*. San Francisco: Jossey-Bass.

Carnevale, A. (1989). "Workplace Basics: The Skills Employers Want." *AACJC Journal*, February/March, pp. 29-33.

Carnevale, A. & Carnevale, E. (1994). "Growth Patterns in Workplace Training." *Training and Development* 48, pp. 22-28.

Carnevale, A. & Ferman, L. (Eds.) (1990). *New Developments in Worker Training: A Legacy for the 1990s*. Madison, WI: Industrial Relations Research Association.

Carnevale, A., Gainer, L. J. & Villet, J. (1990). *Training in America: The Organization and Strategic Role of Training*. San Francisco: Jossey-Bass Publishers.

Castells, Manuel (1992). *Four Asian Tigers with A Dragon Head: A Comparative Analysis of the State, Economy, and Society in the Asian Pacific Rim*. In R. Appelbaum & J. Henderson (Eds.) *States and Development in the Asian Pacific Rim*, pp. 33-70. Newbury Park: Sage.

CEDEFOP (1992). *Continuing Education and Training of the Long Term Unemployed in 10 Member States of the European Community*. Summary Report. Lanham: UNIPUB.

Chalmers, N. J. (1994). "Retraining Under Conditions of Restructuring: Japan." *Training Policy Study*, No. 6. Geneva: ILO.

Chan, William (1993). "Retraining the Unemployed in Hong Kong." *HKCER Letters*, Hong Kong Centre for Economic Research.

Cheung, Jacqueline Tak-york (1994). *Models of Workplace Learning*. Unpublished Master of Education Thesis. Vancouver: University British Columbia.

Clark, Donald M. (1983). *Displaced Workers: A Challenge for Vocational Education.* Columbus Center on Education and Training for Employment.

Cohen, Robin (1987). "Theorizing International Labour." In R. E. Boyd et al. (Eds.) *International Labour and the Third World: The Making of a New Working Class,* pp. 3-25. Aldershot: Gower.

Conklin, David W. (1989). *Information Technology: Globalization, Diffusion, Innovation and Retraining.* London, Ontario: University of Western Ontario.

Construction Industry Training Authority (1993). *Annual Report, 1992-93.* Hong Kong: CITA.

Cook, Sarah (1994). *Training for Empowerment.* Brookfield: Ashgate.

Courchene, Melanie (1991). *Training, Retraining, and Labour Market Adjustment.* Kingston: Queen's University, Industrial Relations Center.

Cyert, R. M. & Mowery, D. C. (Eds.) (1988). *The Impact of Technological Change on Employment and Economic Growth.* Cambridge: Ballinger.

Dalglish, C.(1984). *Adult Education in Hong Kong.* Paper presented in National Institute of Continuing Education.

David-Wilson, J. (1992). *Workplace Educational/Training Programs in Manufacturing: Employee Perception.* Unpublished M. Ed. Thesis, University of York, Toronto.

Davies, J. B. & MacDonald, G. M. T. (1984). *Information in the Labour Market: Job-Worker Matching and Its Implications for Education in Ontario.* Ontario: University of Toronto Press.

Dennis, H. (1988). *Fourteen Steps in Managing An Aging Work Force.* Lexington: Lexington Books.

Dewar, S. "Total Worker Involvement at Toyota." In Mark Anstey (Ed.) *Worker Participation: South African Options and Experience.* Kenwyn: Juta.

Deutsch, S. (1989). "Worker Learning in the context of changing technology and work environment." In Leymann & Kornbluh (Eds.) *Socialization and Learning at Work,* pp. 237-255. Vermont: Gower.

Disney, R. (1984). "The Regional Impact of Unemployment Insurance in the United States." *Oxford Bulletin of Economics and Statistics,* 46(3), pp. 241-254.

Doeringer, P. B. & Vermeulen, B. (1981). *Jobs and Training in the 1980s: Vocational Policy and the Labor Market.* Boston: Martinus Nijhoff Publishing.

Dunk, Thomas & McBride, Stephen (1996). *The Training Trap: Ideology, Training and the Labour Market.* Winnipeg: Fernwood.

Dunlop, John T. (1992). "The Challenge of Human Resources Development." *Industrial Relations,* 31(1), Winter, pp. 50-55.

Employees Retraining Board (1993). *Progress Report on Employees Retraining Scheme.* Paper presented to the Legislative Council, Hong Kong, March 1993.

Employees Retraining Board (1993). *Progress Report on Employees Retraining Scheme.* Paper presented to the Legislative Council, Hong Kong, June 1993.

Employees Retraining Board (1993). *Progress Report on Employees Retraining Scheme.* Paper presented to the Legislative Council, Hong Kong, November 1993.

Employees Retraining Board (1993-94). *Course Content.* July-August, 1993, January 1994.

Employees Retraining Board (1994). *Employees Retraining Scheme Rules.* January 1994. Hong Kong: Government Printer.

European Centre for the Development of Vocational Training (1983). *New Perspectives in Continuing Education and Training in the European Community — Seminar Report.* Berlin: Author.

Evans, Brendan (1992). *The Politics of the Training Market.* New York: Routledge.

Faddis, Constance (1983). *Retraining and Upgrading Workers: A Guide for Postsecondary Educators.* Columbus Center on Education and Training for Employment.

Ferman, L. A., Hoyman, M., Cutcher-Gershenfeld, J. & Savoie, E. J. (1990). *New Developments in Worker Training: A Legacy for the 1990s.* Madison: Industrial Relations Research Association.

Ferman, Louis A. (1991). *Joint Training Program: A Union-Management Approach to Preparing Workers for the Future.* Ithaca, New York: ILR Press.

Forrester, Keith (1995). *Workplace Learning Perspectives on Education, Training and Work.* Brookfield: Ashgate.

Frazis, Harley J. (1995). "Employer-Provided Training: Results from a New Survey." *Monthly Labour Review,* 118, pp. 3-17.

Frobel, Folker (1980). *New International Division of Labour: Structural Unemployment in Industrialized Countries and Industrialization in Developing Countries.* London: Cambridge University Press.

Fryer, B. (1990). "The Challenge to Working-Class Education." In B. Simon (Ed.) *The Search for Enlightenment.* London: Lawrence & Wishart.

Furaker, Bengt & Lief, Johansson (1990). "Unemployment and Labour Market Policies in the Scandinavian Countries." *Acta Sociologica*, 33(2), pp. 141-164.

Gladstone, A. & Ozaki, M. (1991). *Working Together*. Geneva: International Labour Office.

Gleeson, J., McPhee, J. & Spatz, L. (1988). "Training Needs of Supervisors and Middle Managers." *Work and People*, 13(3), pp. 32-36.

Gordus, Jeanne P. (1987). *Preventing Obsolescence Through Retraining: Contexts, Policies and Programs*. Columbus Center on Education & Training for Employment.

Gospel, Howard F. (1990). *Industrial Training and Technological Innovation: A Comparative and Historical Study*. New York: Routledge.

Gottschalk, Peter (1983). *U.S. Labor Market Policies Since the 1960s*. Madison: University of Wisconsin.

Government of Canada (1991). *Learning Well....Living well*. Consultation Paper.

Grayson, J. P. (1986). *Plant Closures and De-skilling: Three Case Studies. An Analysis of Skills, Wages, and Retraining of Former Employees of SKF Canada Ltd., Scarborough; CGE, Scarborough; and Black and Decker, Barrie*. Ottawa: Science Council of Canada.

Hall, K. & Miller, I. (1975). *Retraining and Tradition*. New York: Routledge, Chapman & Hill.

Harlan, S. L. & Steinberg, R. J. (Eds.) (1989). *Job Training for Women: The Promise and Limits of Public Policies*. Philadelphia: Temple University Press.

Herschback, Dennis R. (1984). *Addressing Vocational Training and Retraining Through Educational Technology: Policy Alternatives.* Columbus Center on Education & Training For Employment.

Hellyer, M.R. & Schulman, B. (1989). "Workers' Education." In S.B. Merriam & Cunningham, P.M. (Eds.), *Handbook of Adult and Continuing Education,* pp. 569-583. San Francisco: Jossey-Bass Publishers.

Henderson, J. & Castells, M. (1987) (Eds.) *Global Restructuring and Territorial Development.* Newbury Park: Sage.

Henderson, J. & Cohen, R. (1982). "On the Reproduction of the Relations of Production." In Ray Forest et al. (Eds.) *Social Theory and Urban Political Economy.* Aldershot: Gower.

Hendry, C. (1990). "New Technology, New Careers: The Impact of Flexible Specialization on Skills and Jobs." *New Technology, Work and Employment,* 5(1), pp. 31-43.

Hill, Richard C. (1987). "Global Factory and Company Town: The Changing Division of Labour in the International Automobile Industry." In J. Henderson & M. Castells (Eds.) *Global Restructuring and Territorial Development,* pp. 18-37. Newbury Park: Sage.

Hodson, D. (1994). "Training in the Workplace: Continuity and Change." *Sociological Perspectives,* Spring.

Hollenbeck, K., Pratzer, F. C. & Rosen, H. (Eds.) (1984). *Displaced Workers: Implications for Educational and Training Institutions.* Columbus: Ohio State University.

Hong Kong Confederation of Trade Unions (1992). *CTU in Solidarity,* September, Hong Kong.

Hong Kong Confederation of Trade Unions (1993). *Turning Point,* January, 1994, Hong Kong.

Hong Kong Government (1992). *Employees Retraining Ordinance*, Chapter 423, December 4, Hong Kong.

Hong Kong Government (1990-96). *Hong Kong Annual Reports*. Hong Kong: Government Printer.

Hong Kong Government (1996). *Review of the Employees Retraining Scheme: A Consultation Paper*. Hong Kong: Education and Manpower Branch.

Hong Kong Legislative Council (1992-94). *Minutes*, Hong Kong.

Hong Kong Productivity Council (1993-94). *Productivity News*. All Issues. Hong Kong: Productivity Council.

Hughes, Christina & Tight, Malcolm (1995). "The Myth of the Learning Society." *British Journal of Educational Studies*, 43(3), pp. 290-304.

Human Resources Development Canada (1994). *Agenda: Jobs and Growth. Improving Social Security in Canada. A Discussion Paper*. Ottawa: Minister of Supply and Services.

Hutchins, David (1985). *Quality Circles Handbook*. London: Pitman Publishing Co.

International Labor Office (1983). *Training and Retraining of Men and Women in the Metal Trades With Special Reference to Technological Changes Report*. Washington, D.C.: International Labor Office.

International Labor Office (1990). *The Role of Public Employment Services in the Manpower Redeployment Process*. Labour Administration Branch Document No. 19. Geneva.

International Labor Office (1990). *Training Needs Assessment and Monitoring*. Washington, D.C.: International Labor Office.

International Labor Office (1991). *The Impact of Technological Change on Work and Training.* Tripartite European Meeting on the Impact of Technological Change on Work and Training. TRITEC/1991/1. Geneva.

International Labor Office (1991). *Workers' Education in Action: Selected Articles from Labor Education.* Geneva: International Labor Office.

International Labor Office (1992). *Adjustment and Human Resources Development.* Report VI. International Labour Conference, 79th Session. Geneva.

International Labor Office (1993). *Consequences of Structural Adjustment for Employment, Training, Further Training and Retraining in the Metal Trades.* Report II. Metal Trades Committee, Thirteenth Session. Geneva.

International Labor Office (1995). *World Labor Report 1995. Controversies in Labour Statistics, Ageing Societies — Problems and Prospects for Older Workers.* Washington, D.C.: International Labor Office.

International Personnel Management Association (1989). *Readings on Perspectives in Training.* Alexandria, VA: IPMA.

Islam, Rizwanul (Ed.) (1994). *Social Dimensions of Economic Reforms in Asia.* New Delhi: International Labor Organization.

Janoski, Thomas (1994). "Direct State Intervention in the Labor Market: The Explanation of Active Labor Market Policy from 1950 to 1988 in Social Democratic, Conservative, and Liberal Regimes." In Thomas Janoski & Alexander Hicks (Eds.) *The Comparative Political Economy of the Welfare State*, pp. 54-92. Cambridge: Cambridge University Press.

Jarvis, Peter (1986). *Sociological Perspectives on Lifelong Education and Lifelong Learning.* Athens, Georgia: University of Georgia.

Jarvis, Peter (1995). *Adult and Continuing Education: Theory and Practice.* London: Routledge.

Jorgensen, Henning & Lind, Jens (1987). "Decentralized Welfare Capitalism: The Case of Employment and Industrial Policies." *Acta Sociologica*, 30(3-4), pp. 313-37.

Khan, M. (Ed.) (1987). *Labour Administration: Profile on Hong Kong*. Bangkok: International Labour Office.

Knowles, M. (1980). *From Pedagogy to Andragogy*. Chicago: Follett Publishing Company.

Kolberg, W. H. (Ed.) (1983). *The Dislocated Worker: Preparing America's Work Force For New Jobs*. Cabin John: Sevens Locks Press for the National Alliance of Business.

Koppel, Ross & Hoffman, Alice (1996). "Dislocation Policies in the USA: What Should We Be Doing?" *Annals of the American Academy of Political and Social Science*, 544, pp. 111-126.

Kornbluh, H. & Greene, R.T. (1989). "Learning, Empowerment, and Participative Work Process." In H. Leymann & H. Kornbluh (Eds.), *Socialization and Learning at Work*, pp. 256-274. Aldershot: Avebury.

Krueger, Anne (1995). "East Asian Experience and the Endogenous Growth Theory." In Takatoshi Ito & Anne Krueger (Eds.) *Growth Theories in Light of the East Asian Experience*, pp. 9-36. Chicago: University of Chicago Press.

Kurian, G.T. (1992). *Encyclopedia of the Third World*. New York: Facts on File.

Lai Chi Kok Labour Group (1993). *Survey on Employees Retraining*. Hong Kong: Author.

Lanbury, R. & Ng, S.H. (1992). "Human Resources Development in China and Hong Kong: A Comparative Perspective." In Edward Chen (Ed.) *Labour-Management Relations in the Asia-Pacific Region*. Hong

Kong: Centre of Asian Studies, University of Hong Kong.

Layard, Richard (1986). *How to Beat Unemployment*. New York: Oxford.

Leigh, Duane E. (1990). *Does Training Work for Displaced Workers? A Survey of Existing Evidence*. Kalamazoo, Michigan: W. E. Upjohn Institute for Employment Research.

Leigh, Duane E. (1992). *Retraining Displaced Workers: What can Developing Countries Learn from OECD Nations?* Policy Research Working Paper No. 946. Washington, D.C.: World Bank.

Leigh, Duane E. (1994). *Retraining displaced workers: The US experience*. Training Policy Study No. 1. Geneva: International Labor Office.

Leigh, Duane E. (1995). *Assisting Workers Displaced By Structural Change*. Kalamazoo, Michigan: W. E. Upjohn Institute for Employment Research.

Leung, Po-leung et al. (Eds.) (1990-Present). *Labor Movement Monthly*. Hong Kong: Employment Union.

Levitan, S. A. & Gallo, F. (1988). *A Second Chance: Training for Jobs*. Kalamazoo, Michigan: W. E. Upjohn Institute for Employment Research.

Leymann, H. (1989a). "Learning Theories." In H. Leymann & H. Kornbluh (Eds.) *Socialization and Learning At Work*. Aldershot: Avebury.

Leymann, H. (1989b). "Towards a New Paradigm of Learning in Organization." In H. Leymann & H. Kornbluh (Eds.) *Socialization and Learning at Work*. Aldershot: Avebury.

Lillard, L. A. & Tan, H. W. (1986). *Private Sector Training: Who Gets It and What Are Its Effects?* Rand Publication.

Lofberg A. (1989). "Learning and Educational Intervention from a

Constructivist Point of View." In H. Leymann & H. Kornbluh (Eds.) *Socialization and Learning At Work*. Aldershot: Avebury.

Lucas, Robert E. (1994). "The Impact of Structural Adjustment on Training Needs." *International Labour Review*, 133(5-6), pp. 677-94.

Lui, T. L. (1994). *Wage Work at Home: The Social Organization of Industrial Outwork in Hong Kong*. Brookfield: Ashgate.

Narsick, Victoria J. (Ed.) (1987). *Learning in the Workplace*. Kent, UK: Croom Helm.

Marsick, Victoria J. (1988a). "Learning in the Workplace: The Case for Reflectivity and Critical Reflectivity." *Adult Education Quarterly* 38(4), pp. 187-198.

Marsick, Victoria J. (1988b). *Enhancing Staff Development in Diverse Settings*. San Francisco: Jossey-Bass.

Marsick, V. J. & Watkins, K. (1990). *Informal and Incidental Learning in the Workplace*. New York: Routledge.

Mezirow, Jack (1991). *Transformative Dimension of Adult Learning*. San Francisco: Jossey-Bass.

Miller, Isabel (1975). *Retraining and Tradition: Skilled Worker in An Era of Change*. Woodstock Boohman Publisher.

Mincer, J. (1989). *Job Training: Costs, Returns and Wage Profiles*. Cambridge: National Bureau of Economic Research.

Mok, Tai Kei (1977). *Labour Education Programs for Young Industrial Workers in Hong Kong — A Preliminary Program Evaluation of Three Voluntary Agencies*. Unpublished Master of Social Work Dissertation, University of Hong Kong.

Morgan, Ronald R. (1997). *Enhancing Learning in Training and Adult*

Education. Westport: Greenwood Press.

Mort, Margaret (1985). *Retraining for the Elderly Disabled.* New York: Routledge, Chapman & Hall.

Muszynski, L. & Wolfe, D. A. (1989). "New Technology and Training: Lessons from Abroad." *Canadian Public Policies,* 15(3), pp. 245-264.

Myles, J. & Fawcett, G. (1990). *Job Skills and the Service Economy.* Ottawa: Economic Council of Canada.

Ng, Shek Hong (1987). "Training Problems and Challenges in a Newly Industrializing Economy: The Case of Hong Kong." *International Labour Review,* 126, pp. 467-78.

Ng, Shek Hong (1990). "Labour and Employment." In R. Wong & Joseph Cheng (Eds.) *The Other Hong Kong Report 1990,* pp. 267-296. Hong Kong: Chinese University of Hong Kong Press.

Ng, Shek Hong (1994). "The Role of the Government In Human Resources Development: Retrospect and Prospect." In Benjamin K. P. Leung & Teresa Y. C. Wong (Eds.) *25 Years of Social and Economic Development in Hong Kong,* pp. 458-88. Hong Kong: University of Hong Kong Press.

Niland, John (1974). "Retraining Problems of An Active Manpower Policy." *Australian Economic Papers* 13(23), December, pp. 159-170.

Olsen, G. M. (Ed.) (1988). *Industrial Change and Labour Market Adjustment in Sweden and Canada.* Toronto: Garamond Press.

Organization for Economic Co-operation & Development (1983). *The Future of Vocational Education and Training.* Paris: OECD.

Organization for Economic Co-operation & Development (1990). *Labour Market Policies for the 1990s.* Paris: OECD.

Organization for Economic Co-operation & Development (1996). *Lifelong Learning for All*. Paris: OECD.

Pang, Eng-Fong & Linda Yim, Y. C. (1989). "High Tech and Labour in the Asian NICs." *Labour and Society*, 14, pp. 43-57.

Payne, J. (1990). "Effectiveness of Adult Off-the-Job Skills Training." *Employment Gazette*, 98(3), pp. 143-149.

Pearson, Richard (1984). *Training and Employment*. Brookfield: Ashgate.

Pettersen, Per Arnt (1976). "Parliamentary Attitudes Toward Labor Market Policies." *European Journal of Political Research*, 4, pp. 399-420.

Picot, G. (1987). *Unemployment and Training*. Ottawa: Statistics Canada.

Picot, G., Myles, J. & Wannell, T. (1990). *Good Jobs/Bad Jobs and the Declining Middle: 1967-1986*. Ottawa: Statistics Canada.

Poon, Theresa (1992). "New Technology and the Notions of Technological Determinism, Managerial Strategies and Social Choice — Where Does Hong Kong Fit In?" In Edward Chen (Ed.) *Labour Management Relations in the Asia-Pacific Region*. Hong Kong: Centre of Asian Studies, University of Hong Kong.

Prais, S. J. (1995). *Productivity and Training: Facts and Policies in International Perspective*. New York: Cambridge University Press.

Rainbird, Helen (1990). *Training Matters: Union Perspectives on Industrial Restructuring and Training*. Cambridge: Blackwell.

Rajan, A. & Grilo, E. M. (1990). *Vocational Training Scenarios for Some Member States of the European Community: A Synthesis Report for France, Greece, Italy, Portugal, Spain and the United Kingdom*. Berlin: European Centre for the Development of Vocational Training.

Ravid, G. (1987). "Self-Directed Learning in Industry." In V. Marsick (Ed.)

Learning in the Workplace, pp. 101-118. New York: Croom Helm.

Reagan, P. B. (1984). *Alternatives for On-the-Job Training*. Ohio: Ohio State University.

Reissert, Bernd (1991). "The Regional Impact of Unemployment Insurance and Active Labour Market Policy: An International Comparison." In Werner Sengenberger & Duncan Campbell (Eds.) *Creating Economic Opportunities: The Role of Labour Standards in Industrial Restructuring*, pp. 117-136. Geneva: International Institute for Labour Studies.

Riddell, W. C. (1993). *Evaluation of Manpower and Training Programs: The North American Experience*. Vancouver: University of British Columbia.

Risk, R. C. (1986). *Finding Work: Cross National Perspectives on Employment and Training*. London: Farmer Press.

Robson, R. T. (Ed.) (1984). *Employment and Training R & D: Lessons Learned and Future Directions*. Kalamazoo: W. E. Upjohn Institute for Employment Research.

Rosefeld, Stuart (1986). *Vocational Education and Economic Growth: Connections and Conundrums*. Columbus Center on Education and Training for Development.

Rosow, J. M. & Zager, R. (1988). *Training -- The Competitive Edge: Introducing New Technology into the Workplace*. San Francisco: Jossey-Bass Publishers.

Rubenson, K. (1989). "The Sociology of Adult Education." In S.B. Merriam & Cunningham, P.M. (Eds.), *Handbook of Adult and Continuing Education*, pp. 51-69. San Francisco: Jossey Bass.

Rubenson, K. & Schutze, G. (1992). *Learning At and Through the Workplace — A Review of Participation and Adult Learning Theory*. Vancouver: University of British Columbia.

Ryan, Paul (1991). *International Comparisons of Vocational Education and Training*. Bristol: Taylor & Francis.

Sah, A. K. (1991). *Systems Approach to Training and Development*. Eliot Apt Books.

Salome, Bernard & Charmes, Jacques (1988). *In-Service Training: Five Asian Experiences*. Washington, D.C.: Organization of Economic Co-operation and Development.

Sarmiento, A. R. & Kay, A. (1990). *Worker-centered Learning: A Union Guide to Workplace Literacy*. Washington, D.C.: AFL-CIO Human Resources Development Institute.

Scarpetta, S., Boeri, T. & Reutersward, A. (1993). *Unemployment Benefit Systems and Active Labour Market Policies in Central and Eastern Europe: An Overview*. Paris: OECD, Centre for Co-operation with the Economies in Transition.

Scott, Ian (1989). *Political Change and the Crisis of Legitimacy of Hong Kong*. Hawaii: University of Hawaii Press.

Schmid, Gunter, Reissert, Bernd & Brache, Gert (1992). *Unemployment Insurance and Active Labor Market Policy*. Detroit: Wayne State University.

Seitchik, Adam & Zornitsky, Jeffrey (1989). *From One Job to the Next: Worker Adjustment in a Changing Labor Market*. Kalamazoo, Michigan: W. E. Upjohn Institute for Employment Research.

Sengenberger, Werner & Campbell, Duncan (Eds.) (1994). *Creating Economic Opportunities: The Role of Labour Standards in Industrial Restructuring*. Geneva: International Institute for Labour Studies.

Senker, P. (1989). "Technical Change, Work Organization and Training: Some Issues Relating to the Role of Market Forces." *New Technology, Work and Employment*, 4(1), pp. 48-55.

Shackleton, J.R. (1992). *Training Too Much?* London: Institute of Economic Affairs.

Sharpe, A. (1990). "Training the Workforce: A Challenge Facing Canada in the 1990s." *Perspectives*, Winter, pp. 21-31.

SHRM (1989). *SHRM Training — Retraining Survey Report.* Alexandria Society for Human Resources Management.

Simmons, Colin & Kalantaridis, Christos (1995). "Labour Regimes and the Domestic Domain: Manufacturing Garments in Rural Greece." *Work, Employment and Society*, Vol. 9, No.2, pp. 287-308.

Simpson, W. (1983). An Economic Analysis of Industrial Training in Canada. Ottawa: Economic Council of Canada.

Siu, K.F. & Luk, Y.F. (1990). "The State of the Economy." In Richard Wong & Joseph Cheng (Eds.) *The Other Hong Kong Report 1990*, pp. 205-20. Hong Kong: Chinese University of Hong Kong Press.

Skold, M. (1989). "Everyday Learning: The Basis for Adult Education." In H. Leymann & H. Kornbluh (Eds.) *Socialization and Learning At Work*. Aldershot: Avebury.

Sobel, D. & Meurer, S. (1988). *A Shameful Silence: Older Workers, New Technology, and Retraining.* Toronto: Labour Council of Metropolitan Toronto.

Sorge, A. (1984). *Technological Change, Employment, Qualifications and Training.* Berlin: European Centre for the Development of Vocational Training.

Staley, Eugene (1971). *Planning Occupational Education and Training for Development.* New York: Praeger.

Stewart, F. (1994). "The new international division of labour," in *World of Work*, No. 8. Geneva: ILO.

Sticht, T.G. & Hickey, D.T. (1991). "Functional Context Theory, Literacy, and Electronics Training." In R.F. Dillion & J.W. Pellegrino (Eds), *Instruction, Theoretical and Applied Perspectives*. New York: Praeger.

Sweet, R. (1988). "Industry Restructuring and Workforce Reskilling." *Work and People*, 13(1-2), pp. 36-39.

Tang, Kwong-leung et al. (Eds.) (1983). *Social Work for Industrial Workers*. Hong Kong: Hong Kong Social Workers' General Union. (In Chinese)

Tang, Kwong-leung et al. (Eds.) (1986). *Social Security and Hong Kong Industrial Workers*. Hong Kong: Joint Labour Council. (In Chinese)

Tang, Kwong-leung & Jacqueline Tak-york Cheung (1996). "Models of Workplace Learning in North America: A Review." *International Journal of Lifelong Education*, 15(4), pp. 256-265.

Taylor, David (1994). *Training for Change Activities to Promote Positive Attitudes to Change*. East Brunswick: Nichols Publishing.

Therborn, Goran (1986). *Why Some Peoples Are More Unemployed Than Others*. London: Verso.

Trade Union Centre (1990-96). *Labour Movement Monthly*. Hong Kong: Christian Industrial Council.

Tso, Wendy (1993). "Training Scheme Gives New Hope to Unemployed." *Hong Kong Industrialist*, pp. 20-21, July.

Turner, H.A. et al. (1980). *The Last Colony: But Whose? A Study of the Labour Movement, Labour Market and Labour Relations in Hong Kong*. Hong Kong: Cambridge University Press.

Turner, H.A., Fosh, P. & Ng, S.H. (1991). *Between Two Societies: Hong Kong Labour In Transition*. Hong Kong: Centre of Asian Studies, University of Hong Kong.

Twentieth Century Fund Staff (1995). *Dislocated Workers: Worker Adjustment and Retraining Notification Act Not Meeting Its Goals.* New York: Twentieth Century Fund/ Priority Press.

Twentieth Century Fund Staff (1996). *No One Left Behind: The Report of the Twentieth Century Fund Task Force on Retraining America's Workforce.* New York: Twentieth Century Fund/Priority Press.

U.S. Department of Labor (1985). *Employment, Hours of Earnings: U.S. 1904-1984.* Bulletin 1312-12, Washington, D.C.: GPO.

Verduin, John R., Jr., Miller, Harry & Greer, Charles (1986). *The Lifelong Learning Experience: An Introduction.* Springfield, Illinois: C.C. Thomas.

Vickers, Margaret (1994). *Skill Standards and Skill Formation: Cross-National Perspectives on Alternate Training Strategies.* Boston: Jobs for the Future.

Villeval, M.-C. (1991). "Labour Market Restructuring and Deprivation Processes," in *Labour and Society,* No. 16/2. Geneva.

Volpert, W. (1989). "Work and Personality Development from the Viewpoint of the Action Regulation Theory." In H. Leymann & H. Kornbluh (Eds.) *Socialization and Learning At Work.* Aldershot: Avebury.

Vroman, W. (1986). *The Funding Crisis in State Unemployment Insurance.* Kalamazoo, Michigan: W. E. Upjohn Institute for Employment Research.

Vroman, W. (1991). *The Decline in Unemployment Insurance Claims Activity in the 1980s.* Washington, D.C.: The Urban Institute.

Walters, Jonathan (1994). "The Truth About Training." *Governing,* 8, pp. 32-35.

Wilson, Graham (1979). *Unions in American National Politics.* New York:

St. Martin's.

Wing, Suen (1994). "Labour and Employment." In Donald H. McMillen & Man, Si-wai (Eds.) *The Other Hong Kong Report 1994*, pp. 149-164. Hong Kong: Chinese University of Hong Kong Press.

Wittich, Gunther (1966). *The German Road to Full Employment.* Unpublished Ph.D. Dissertation. Berkeley: University of California, Berkeley.

Wong, Y.T. (1989). "Hong Kong Labour Relations and Human Resources." Hong Kong: Wide Angle Press. (In Chinese)

Yudd, R. & Smith, D. S. (1990). *The Availability of Information for Defining and Assessing Basic Skills Required for Specific Occupations.* Washington, D.C.: Urban Institute.

Yun, Hing Ai (1995). "Automation and the New Work Patterns: Cases from Singapore's Electronics Industry." *Work, Employment and Society*, Vol.9, No.2, pp. 309-327.

Zacharakis-Jutz & Shied, F.M. (1993). "Workers' Education, Social Construction, and Adult Education." *Adult Education Quarterly*, 43(2), pp. 101-109.

Ziderman, Adrian (1969). "Costs and Benefits of Adult Retraining in the United Kingdom." *Economica*, 36(144), November, pp. 363-376.

**Recent Reports, Press Releases, Studies and Speeches
On Employees Retraining Scheme and Retraining**

1.   *Hong Kong Annual Report 1997*, April 1997, Hong Kong Government

2.   *Proposals to Revamp Employees Retraining Scheme*, December 3, 1996, Press Release, Hong Kong Government.

3. *Governor's Policy Address 1996*, October 2, 1996, Governor Christopher Patten.

4. *Employment: Policy Commitments*, October 1996, Mr. Joseph Wong, Secretary for Education and Manpower.

5. *Hong Kong Into the 21st Century: The Servicing Economy*, March 12, 1996, Mr. Donald Tsang, Financial Secretary.

6. *Budget Speech 1996-97*, March 6, 1996, Mr. Donald Tsang, Financial Secretary.

7. *Public Consultation on Discrimination*, January 24, 1996, Press Release, Hong Kong Government.

8. *Governor's Summit Meeting On Employment*, November 9, 1995.

9. *Paradoxes Make Hong Kong Tick*, Speech to the Harvard Business School Association on October 13, 1995, Mrs Anson Chan, Chief Secretary.

10. *Supplementary Labour Scheme: A Good Decision*, October 12, 1995, Mr. T. H. Chau, Acting Financial Secretary.

11. *The Governor's Policy Address 1995*, October 11, 1995, Governor Christopher Patten.

12. *Progress Report 1995*, October 9, 1995, Mrs. Anson Chan, Chief Secretary.

13. *Majority Have Confidence in Hong Kong's Future*, October 5, 1995, Survey Report, Home Affairs Branch, Hong Kong Government.

14. *Setting Out Priorities*, Economic Strategy Speech to the Legislative Council on June 14, 1995, Mr. T. H. Chau, Acting Financial Secretary.

15. *Budget Speech 1995-96*, March 6, 1995, Mr. Donald Tsang, Financial Secretary.

♦ ♦ ♦

INDEX

Employees Retraining Scheme,
  Course Content, 86, 115
  Course Delivery, 73, 86, 88
  Course Objective, 85
  Instruction Method, 86
  needs assessment, 85, 118
  Programming, 52, 56, 83, 84, 93
  Training of Instructors, 87
extensive pauperization, 52

F
female labor, 49
First Opium War, 33
Frankel, Stephen, 59, 60
free market, 32
Fryer, B., 29, 115
Functional Context Theory, 16, 29, 127

G
General Labor Importation Scheme, vi
Goldstein, H., 28
Greene, R., 29, 30, 120
Guangdong, 50-51
Guangdong Women's Association, 51
Gutkind, Peter, 59

H
Habermas' theory of communication competence, 19
Hellyer, M., 28, 117
Henderson, Jeffrey, 50, 59, 60, 112, 117
Henderson and Castells, 59, 60
Hickey, D. T., 29, 127
Hill, Richard C., 60, 116, 117
Hong Kong
  Census and Statistics Department, 61, 104
  Clothing Industry Workers' General Union, 83
  Colony, 6, 33, 35, 37, 44, 47, 50, 52, 79, 81, 82, 89, 128

Confederation of Trade Unions, 83, 96, 97, 117
economic development, 6, 9, 34, 60, 82, 83, 123
economic history, 31-36
Education and Manpower Committee, 63
government, v, vi, 6, 7, 55, 58-60, 81, 84, 89, 96, 97, 99, 100, 118, 130, 131
investment in China, 51
Labour Department, 36, 38, 63, 64, 80, 93, 104
Legislative Council, 55, 59, 76, 118
Legislature, 47, 48, 55, 109
Local Employment Service, 40, 93, 104
manufacturing industries, 34, 51, 64
Productivity Council, 71, 118
Seamen's Union, 71
Welfare Policy, 82
human capital, 44, 91
human resources development, 9, 60, 89, 114, 118-120, 123, 126

I
in-service training, 35, 36, 42-44, 58, 126
Indonesia, 50
industrial restructuring, 3, 42, 109, 111, 124-126
instrumental learning, 19, 75
International Division of Labor, vi, 49-52
internationalization of labor, 51

J
Job Matching Programme, 92, 93

K
Knowles, M., 10, 16, 120

◆   ◆   ◆

MELLEN STUDIES IN BUSINESS